"Medicine's hi

MW00414471

Radiologists at Work

Saving Lives with the Lights Off

X-ray Visions Series - Boxed Set

Carolyn Jourdan

The names of the physicians who contributed to this book are listed at the end. The names of the doctors in individual stories have been changed, as well as certain other identifying features, to protect the privacy of both physician and patient.

softcover ISBN 9780997201215
ebook ISBN 9780989930437

Formatting by Polgarus Studio www.polgarusstudio.com

Pulvis et umbra sumus
We are but dust and shadow
Horace

Contents

Prologue

This book is the product of interviews with twenty radiologists from more than half a dozen subspecialties. It covers a period of over seventy years of practice, from the 1940s to the present day.

The doctors I spoke to are mostly from the southeast, so their experiences bear the distinctive stamp of the famous, or infamous, charity hospitals in big southern cities, as well as the isolated and insular Southern Highlands.

Radiological training is long and arduous, and the path is not always straight or smooth. This book includes vignettes about defining moments of childhood, life-altering experiences in the military, and chaotic stints in the emergency room, as well as traditional radiological tasks.

The settings run the gamut from humble general practice encounters with snake handlers in deepest darkest Appalachia to the glamor of treating the most confounding cases with cutting edge technologies in world famous research hospitals.

The book ends with first hand accounts of unexpected cures in what were thought to be hopeless situations where even the most fearsome technology was stumped, and then trumped, by a miracle.

I've spent fifty-four years being fascinated with x-rays—ever since the day a medical school classmate of my father's hoisted me up into the pilot's seat of a fighter jet and then showed me the radiology reading room where he was doing his residency—forever lending an aura of the utmost glamour and adventure to the world of radiology.

Because I was only six when these events took place, for many years afterwards I thought all radiologists were fighter pilots, too.

I grew up in a rural family doctor's office and worked there off and on for many years. My father was a solo practitioner in East Tennessee, next door to the Great Smoky Mountains. I watched him read his patients' x-rays for forty years until he retired.

After that I spent another fifteen years intermittently shadowing radiologists— not literally producing any shadows of course, since these doctors work in the dark.

In the span of a single human lifetime, the practice of radiology has morphed beyond recognition. The hands-on working environment of a World War II generation doctor has been utterly transformed by vast technological advancements.

Rigid adaptations are being imposed on physicians by the increasing dominance of technology—and no doctors are more affected by this than radiologists.

Seventy years ago these specialists took their own x-rays and carried them into a darkroom where they developed the images by hand. They hung the wet films on a line with clothespins and read them while they were still dripping.

The new medical imaging technologies have led to segmentation of radiology into subspecialties and this, in turn, has given rise to an army of technicians who operate the complex machinery.

The day-to-day tasks of radiologists have become progressively more refined and rarefied, and not necessarily for the better. Doctors are finding themselves forced to serve their machines in a way that resembles something out of science fiction.

Today a radiologist might sit alone in the dark for a twelve-hour shift, dictating to a voice recognition system as he reads images from an emergency room on the other side of the world.

The pace of the work has continued to increase as well. Machines have automated or even alleviated humble tasks like developing and displaying x-rays, and at the same time greatly advanced diagnostics and treatment, but they've also dehumanized the workplace.

Diagnostic radiologists, for example, are tasked with interpreting *far* more images than before, a virtual tsunami of visual data, while their body movements are progressively more restricted.

These highly trained seers are well paid, but they're increasingly isolated from their peers. They hardly move while their eyes flicker rapidly around the area bounded by a single black and white image on a computer.

Thousands of images flow past. And they dare not miss anything.

This book is a tribute to the secret lives of radiologists. I hope you'll enjoy this behind the scenes look at doctors who work behind the scenes.

Although you will rarely, if ever, meet any of them, these hidden heroes are back there somewhere at the end of a long hallway, sitting alone in a dark room saving lives with the lights off.

CHASING SHADOWS
The Good Old Days

Radiologists are relative newcomers to the ancient art of medicine. The first radiograph was made, by accident, a hundred and twenty five years ago.

For hundreds of years before x-rays came on the scene the word physic, *or* physick, *meant treating a patient. Only recently did* physics *come to mean the study of matter and energy and the relationship between them.*

Radiology involves both meanings of the word. Radiologists are physicians who use physics to physic patients' physiques.

The radiology department has always housed the most complicated and dangerous machinery in the hospital. Several of the doctors I spoke to began practice shortly after World War II. They described the cutting edge equipment of the 1940s.

Night Visions

Dr. Goldsmith

"Radiologists used to be called *shadow readers*. There was a good reason for the nickname. Seventy years ago, fifty years ago, the quality of our images was a lot lower.

"We worked with the black and white images most people think of when you say *x-ray*. Nowadays we call those *plain films* to distinguish them from the other types of images that are still produced on transparent film stock, like CTs and MRIs.

"Plain films look kind of like very large photographic negatives, and they used to be developed the same way—in a darkroom. A darkroom could be an appealing working environment for certain types of people.

"It was common to employ the blind in large volume facilities like a big city hospital. We had a blind girl who worked in ours, and a black guy who was a cross dresser. They did wonderful work.

"Back then silver was used to produce the images. Silver metal. This was one of the reasons x-rays were expensive to make and why we usually made only one copy of a film. It wasn't like now where you can cheaply create as many digital copies as you want.

"Old x-rays were valuable. Recyclers could extract the silver from them and they'd give it back to us in the form of ingots! I still have a chunk of silver from a batch of recycled films.

"When I think back on those early images I can't help but wonder, *How in the world did I read them?* They were a lot better than nothing, but the quality wasn't great.

"I really had to have a lot of nerve to come up with an opinion about the images we produced with that crude level of technology, but at the time it seemed wonderful.

"We were *thrilled* that we didn't need to do exploratory surgery on patients as often as we'd had to before. Now we could see inside people without cutting them open! We could see *through* them. That was a huge improvement.

"The invention of the fluoroscope was another major breakthrough. We'd never been able to see *movement* inside a person before. Now we could check for disordered motion. We could see what was going on in a person who was having trouble swallowing, for example.

"You could hand the patient a radio-opaque pill or ask them to drink some radio-opaque liquid and watch them try to swallow it and see what happened.

It was a tremendous new tool, but there were a few problems with the early technology.

"The biggest concern was that you had to be very quick with the fluoroscope because it bombards the patient with radiation when it's turned on. For the patient's safety you have to work really fast.

"Another drawback was that there was no way to record the images—no instant replays. You got one chance to read the picture, *live*, and that was it.

"A third issue was that the early fluoroscopes didn't have any image intensification. There were no separate monitors to amplify what we were seeing. We had to look at the fluoroscope itself to try to understand what was going on.

"Unfortunately the images were so faint you couldn't make them out using your central vision. Even with fully adapted night vision, the only way you could read the fluoro screen was with your peripheral vision.

"You would never read x-rays with your peripheral vision because x-rays are well lit from behind by the lightbox, and your central vision is best for seeing sharp outlines and color.

"Your peripheral vision works better in low light situations. You can't see much detail with it and you can't make out any color, but if there's hardly any light, it's the best vision you have.

"The early fluoroscope screens were so dim you had to be fully accommodated to the dark to see anything on them at all, even with your peripheral vision. And reading the fluoro with your peripheral vision took a *lot* of head movement. You had to look sideways at the screen, swiveling your head all the time, to try to figure out what you were seeing.

Good to Know
Forgotten, But Not Gone

"When you swallow a tablet, you think it's gone. But the chances are it's still in your esophagus. It takes three or four swallows to get a pill all the way down to your stomach. You can't rely on your physical sensation to tell you where it is.

"There is a poor correlation between where a patient thinks something is, where they *feel* it, and where it actually is. We can see things clearly on a fluoroscope and the problem will often be located in a different place than where the patient is pointing.

"Pills like NSAIDS, non-steroidal anti-inflammatories, drugs like aspirin, ibuprofen, Advil, Motrin, or naproxen sodium, Aleve, should be taken with four or five sips of water to make sure they go all the way down. Otherwise they can stay in the esophagus and erode it."

Shadow Operations

Fifty years after my six-year-old brain mistakenly linked fighter pilots and radiologists, I learned that these two careers actually do share an important characteristic. Both require life and death decisions to be made in the dark.

Excellent night vision is crucial for a handful of iconic professions—radiologists, fighter pilots, submarine captains, and astronomers. And, as it turns out, they've learned to make use of each other's gear.

Dr. Myers

"Radiologists have always worked long shifts.

"When you're gonna be on duty for fifteen hours, it's a pain to have to go in half an hour early just so you can sit in a room with the lights off, waiting for your eyes to adapt to the dark, before you can start working.

"Then, if for some reason you have to leave the fluoroscopy suite, every time you go out your night vision gets spoiled, so when you come back you have to wait for another thirty minutes for your eyes to readapt.

"After World War II somebody got the idea that we should wear the same sort of red goggles that aviators wore before their missions. You can find old photos online of pilots wearing them during the briefings before their bombing runs so they'd be fully adapted to the night sky when they got into the cockpit.

"Airplane instruments used to be lit with a variety of colors until somebody figured out that the dark-adaptation of human eyes wasn't ruined by red light. It has to do with the way the rods and cones in your eyes work. They learned to illuminate the airplane's instruments using red light because any other colors destroyed the flight crew's night vision.

"If they used red, the crew would be able to read their instruments and maps and maintain their night vision so they'd be able to see as well as possible during nighttime takeoffs and landings and while flying around in the dark.

"Instruments on submarines were red for this same reason and certain members of the crew wore red goggles there, too, so they'd have fully adapted night vision when they needed to use the periscope at night. After the war it became commonplace for radiologists to use the goggles.

"We'd drive to work in the morning wearing red goggles so we'd be ready to do fluoroscopy when we arrived at the hospital. The goggles looked sorta like sunglasses, except they were huge and red and they sealed around the edges like welding glasses.

"If a car stopped beside you at an intersection, the people would glance over and see this weird creature sitting next to them and do a double take.

"A more worrisome issue was, if you were driving while wearing the goggles, they made it impossible to tell what color the traffic light was, so you had to remember whether the red light was on the top or the bottom of the signal box.

"I wore them when driving to work all during my residency. On my very first trip I was going to Coral Gables Children's Hospital in Homestead when I suddenly realized I couldn't tell whether the light was red or green. That was a bad moment.

"That hospital isn't there anymore. It was destroyed in Hurricane Andrew. Eventually we learned that you could drill a hole in the goggles right over your pupil, and then, by looking through the tiny hole, you could see things you needed to see in the daylight and also read plain films without losing your night vision.

"This was a great improvement because it meant you could drive safely, and also go back and forth between fluoroscopy and reading regular x-rays."

Shady Territory

Dr. Abbott

"When I was reading for more than one hospital, I'd wear the goggles during my drives. That way I could keep my night vision all day long.

"I've always liked to drive too fast, and it was my habit to make one of the runs to a hospital in a nearby town at over ninety miles an hour.

"I got pulled over one day when I was wearing my red goggles over the top of my sunglasses. The cop leaned down and stared at me through the open window. 'What the hell have you got on your face?' he asked.

"I explained that I was a radiologist and was wearing the glasses to protect my night vision. He'd never heard that one before so he let me go without giving me a ticket.

"The next time he pulled me over we recognized each other. I needed to come up with a better excuse, so I told him I was responding to an emergency call. He knew I was lying, but again, he let me go.

"Over time I got to know the two patrolmen who worked that particular stretch of highway and I'd wave at them as I went flying by."

Factoid
Eyeshine

Humans don't see particularly well in the dark compared to nocturnal animals or deep sea creatures. This is because the critters that need to navigate in low light often have an extra layer in the back of their eyes to amplify the ambient illumination.

It's called the *tapetum lucidum,* and it provides enough image intensification that a cat, for example, can see six times better in the dark than a person.

You can tell whether or not a beast has this special layer if you shine a light into its eyes. If they have it you'll see an iridescent reflection called *eyeshine*.

Various species have characteristic colors that shine back at you. In fish the eyeshine is white, in horses it's blue, in cats and dogs it's green. Coyotes, possums, and birds have red eyeshine. Wolf spiders have blue-green. It comes in many colors, even yellow and pink.

Humans and monkeys don't have this structure.

This is particularly unfortunate for radiologists and the nurses and technicians who work with them.

Hitting the Wall

Dr. Scott

"When I first started in fluoroscopy, if you hadn't dark-adapted you couldn't even find the patient in the room!

"Gradually I became familiar with the layout of the suites where we worked and I learned to move around them safely in the dark.

"The radiology technicians had it rough, though. They were the ones who had to come and go from the darkened rooms, escorting patients, and carrying supplies in and out.

"This wasn't easy. Every now and then, especially if there was an emergency and people were running in and out, you'd hear a thud and a crash.

"You knew that meant one of the techs had slammed into a wall in the dark and fallen. I was dark-adapted and could see where the walls were, but the techs couldn't."

Radiological Humor

Dr. Patterson

"Would you like to hear a radiology joke?"

"Sure," I said.

"A technologist emerged from the darkroom, and said, 'I've been assaulted by a radiologist.'

"The other tech said, 'How did you know it was the radiologist? It's dark in there.'

"'I know because he made me do all the work!'"

Two Cooks

Dr. Sullivan

"We wore the red goggles when we went to eat our meals.

"It was extremely nerdy and we got some strange looks, but we needed to do it, so we did.

"I remember wearing them as I was sitting down in the staff cafeteria one evening. The guy at the table next to me leaned over and said, 'We'll eat good tonight!'

"'Why?' I asked. The food at that hospital was terrible.

"'Because the chief cook just shot the assistant cook,' he said. 'One of 'em's in the hospital and other one's in jail!'

"He was right. The people who filled in for the regular cooks were much better. This probably sounds harsh but we were both young and just trying to survive the early years of our training.

"Apparently these kinds of situations aren't that rare. A colleague told me there was a fight in the kitchen at the University of Chicago and the cook bled out before the emergency responders could get there on the hospital's slow elevators.

"They probably should've run down the stairs to get the guy and carried him up to the emergency room instead of trying to bring a resuscitation cart down to him on an elevator, but they didn't think of it in time.

"I don't ever wear them anymore, but I still have my red goggles on a shelf in the closet."

Shooting Myself in the Face

Dr. Hughes

"For a long time when we used the fluoroscope we shot radiation right into our faces with nothing to stop it.

"I did that all through my residency and for years afterwards until we finally got image intensification.

"I had special prescription glasses made with lead shielding. People told me I'd get cataracts, but I didn't.

"My wife, who wasn't around radiological equipment needed cataract surgery though. I think it's because she has blue eyes. My eyes are brown.

"I did so much fluoro I got to the point where I'd toss my radiation badge to the wind. I wanted to do the exams and I knew they'd run me over the permitted level of radiation, so I'd leave my dosimeter on my desk.

"Eventually it got to the point where I'd been x-rayed so many times in those rooms, I decided to switch to MRI to reduce my radiation exposure."

Behind My Back

Dr. Stone

"Things keep changing. My current work environment is unrecognizable from what it used to be when I started out.

"At first I used a two-panel viewer for films. I'd read, dictate, and replace the two films by hand.

"Then for a while I'd read while standing between two techs—one who was loading and the other who was unloading the two light boxes continuously. That went a lot faster because I didn't have to touch the films myself.

"Sometimes I had to read in a room that wasn't exclusively designated for my use. Anything and everything might be going on all around where I was working.

"In that situation I had to learn to concentrate fully. I had to be able to focus in on an image so tightly that I could read and dictate while ignoring incredible noise and distractions going on behind my back.

"I gradually became oblivious to anything but the x-ray."

The Great Radiological Paradox

Dr. Thornton

"There's a fundamental paradox in radiology—radiation can both cure and kill.

"Frequent imaging can catch your tumor, but it can also give you a tumor.

"Radiologists are hardcore scientists. The materials we're dealing with are no joke. Radium, for example, has a half life of over a thousand years.

"We have only a tenth of a millimeter of lead in our protective gear. That's not nearly enough to stop radium.

"When we used radium needles, we didn't dare touch them directly. We worked as quickly as we could and tried to limit our exposure.

"When we brought radium into the hospital, it was in these ominously labeled boxes. Sometimes we used a trolley to transport nuclear materials in heavy lead canisters. People would see us coming and get off the elevator.

"They wouldn't ride with us.

"Most people are surprised to learn that they remain radioactive for a day or two after a nuclear medicine treatment. They don't realize that just because they left the hospital, that doesn't mean the radiation is gone.

"It takes time for it to decay. If your eyes could detect the right wavelength, you'd be able to see that you were still glowing.

"I've been retired for a while now, but sometimes I wonder if I'm still glowing."

The Dungeon

Dr. Roberts

"Radiologists are always trying to reduce glare. Now we have some absolutely black reading rooms—black ceilings, black floors, and black walls. Working in that type of environment affects people differently.

"I'm an outdoor person. I wasn't raised as a mole. Many times I ask myself, *What am I doing in here?*

"I'll get up, go outside, and check to make sure the sun is still shining. You can't sit for eleven hours a day. At least once an hour I get up and walk around.

"You get eye fatigue and you have to take a break. It's good to go for a walk, get a Coke. Then your concentration is better when you come back.

"Radiologists used to move around a lot, doing different procedures, going to different parts of the hospital, but now we're getting more sedentary and more alone.

"I used to perform thirty-five to forty fluoroscopy procedures before noon, moving from one fluoro suite to another. Then I'd stop and read films for a while, going from one reading room to another. I'd alternate like that all day, between doing fluoro and reading plain films.

"I used to be a lot more active than I am now and I interacted with doctors and patients a lot more. But the technology is different now, there is more specialization.

"It's kinda lonely in your dark little room by yourself."

SOLDIERING ON

He that hath the steerage of my course, direct my sail.
William Shakespeare
Romeo and Juliet, Act 1, Scene 4

Paths to becoming a physician often include conflicting elements of fate or destiny. Many doctors were first ordered to become soldiers. Then, when the war was over, they were helped by the military to become healers.

D-Day

Dr. Vincent

"I was seventeen when I got sent to D-Day. I was a foot soldier.

"I wasn't in the first wave, I went in in the afternoon.

"Why the guy who was twenty feet from you was dead and you weren't— I've never figured out.

"During the course of a year I became a staff sergeant and then a second lieutenant because I was the only one left.

"After the war I stayed in the reserves, then a few years later I missed getting sent to Korea by one day.

"I'd transferred from Atlanta to Athens to take a job with the University of Georgia and the very next day after I left they activated the Atlanta unit and sent them to Korea.

"It was just a fluke that I was spared being sent to another war."

Getting Off the First Shot

Dr. Blankenship

"During World War II I was a student at the University of Tennessee in the College of Agriculture. I joined the reserve hoping I'd be able to finish school, but six months later we all got called up.

"I took the military examinations and scored well, so the Army sent me to engineering school in New York. Then, when the war was going badly for the U.S., the Army decided to discontinue the program I was in. The only educational opportunity left was medicine.

"I'd always wanted to be a doctor, but there was no way I could ever have afforded medical school so I'd erased the idea from my mind. Then the military gave me a chance.

"I took another test and passed it, and they sent me to medical training!

"I did pre-med and became a corpsman working in a military hospital inside a prison. This was when penicillin was just coming into vogue and the Army got *all* of it.

"I was told to give a prisoner a shot of the new antibiotic for his gonorrhea. This was the first shot I'd ever given anybody.

"Unfortunately I hurt the guy. The needle curled in his arm and I had trouble getting it out.

"He got pretty irate and threatened my life.

"My very first shot and I got a death threat!"

Backstabbing

Dr. Peterson

"When I was in medical school, just after World War II, there was a *Doctor Draft* which extended for years even after the war was over. I was older, so I got deferred during college and medical school, but then, when I got out, I was assigned to the Navy.

"A couple of guys ahead of me had gotten stuck on a troop transport that went back and forth endlessly from Nova Scotia to England. For two years all they saw was seasickness and broken hands from sailors falling down on the deck of the ship in rough weather.

"I wanted to avoid that, so I enlisted in the Air Force. I was in the military for a total of seven years. I did three years of residency at Jackson Memorial in Miami and then paid back four years.

"In the Air Force everyone had to have a chest x-ray once a year. It was just a frontal view. On one of these routine films, there was a white area in the middle of a guy's spine. 'You have something in your back,' I told him.

"He was a very outgoing man, a cook, a heavy fellow with gold teeth. He told me it was part of a knife. He'd been stabbed in the back and the blade had broken off.

"A piece of metal three or four inches long was still embedded in the soft tissues. It didn't cause the guy any problems, so we left it there.

"In the movies and on television the doctors always have to take out the bullet, or whatever it is. In real life you learn that sometimes these things are best left alone."

Nothing to Nobody

Dr. Moore

"I was planning to be a plastic surgeon, but I got drafted. In the military I was a flight surgeon.

"Aviation medicine involves a lot of *non-patient* medicine. It was a surprise to me, but I discovered that I liked it. Paperwork was easier than dealing with patients.

"So instead of plastic surgery, I ended up in radiology.

"Radiology used to be filled with quiet guys who stayed back in a dark room, but the stereotype of a shy, reserved type of guy no longer fits. There are lots of subspecialties now. We can roam around and do all sorts of things if we want to.

"Some radiologists prefer to stay in the dark, though. They don't wanna do nothing to nobody. They're more academic. They don't wanna have to get in there and fix anything.

"I enjoy fixing things, though, so I became an interventional radiologist."

Lesson From Vietnam

Dr. Carlton

"One thing I learned in Vietnam was that high velocity gunshot injuries are very destructive.

"Another thing I learned was that if a guy was sitting with his back against a tree when he got shot in the stomach, the bark of the tree would end up on the front of the guy.

"That's what happens when the shock wave can't go straight through the person and continue on out the back, but instead is forced to reverse itself and leave the same way it arrived.

"The expansion from the explosion of a high velocity round creates a vacuum. If there's a solid object like a tree behind the person who got shot, the vacuum sucks debris into the wound.

"You end up with bark on the front of the soldier."

Greetings

Dr. Delaney

"I have an identical twin brother. We came from a modest background and had to hitchhike to school every day when we were young. Later we both went to college and worked as dorm janitors to pay for our tuition and books.

"I started out as a baseball player but my career was cut short, so I decided to become a forest ranger. After I'd been studying forestry for a while I noticed I wasn't actually getting to go out into the woods so I started thinking about other careers.

"I liked people and I liked science. So I majored in chemistry, biology, and literature. Then I went to medical school with my brother, and did an internship at Orange County General in Orlando, Florida.

"I planned to become a surgeon, but I got a *Greetings* letter and fourteen days later I was in Vietnam, at an F-4 fighter base.

"I was assigned to a dispensary where I worked as a sort of general practitioner. The only way I was able to get off the base was by taking films to a radiologist.

"I was never anxious to get back to the base, so whenever I took him films I'd sit and watch him while he worked. He was a nice fellow. He'd read x-rays and he'd teach me some stuff.

"After that I decided to become a radiologist.

"Neither of us planned it, but my brother and I both went into the service and then both of us became radiologists."

Hawaii

The Other Dr. Delaney

"I went to college in Tennessee for two years, majoring in Chemistry, and then I got a scholarship to Florida Southern College in Lakeland. In Florida I worked at a cancer research facility. That paid my tuition and gave me one meal a day.

"I didn't have *any* money. I went four or five months without *one penny* in my pocket. I didn't go to any ballgames or on any dates because I had no car and no money.

"I learned to wash my clothes in the shower with Dial soap and shave without shaving cream. Ever since then, for the rest of my life, I've never bought a can of shaving cream. I still shave in the shower. It's a legacy of those days of poverty.

"I have an identical twin brother. He talked me into being a doctor. He was thinking of medicine and we discussed it over the phone. We decided it was academic enough to be stimulating, and we liked helping people.

"Back then doctors were very independent. We both wanted to be able to control our own lives and, from what we saw, nobody told doctors what to do. That was very important to us and a big factor in choosing medicine.

"We both went to medical school at the University of Tennessee in Memphis and then we were drafted at nearly the same time.

"The belief back then was that they wouldn't send you to Vietnam if you were married or if you had children. I wasn't married. I was sent to Bossier City, Louisiana. My brother was married and had a pregnant wife and yet he got sent to Vietnam!

"I interned in Hawaii. There were three hospitals in Honolulu: the Japanese hospital, the Chinese hospital, and Queens, the charity hospital.

"My internship was at Kuakini, the Japanese Hospital. A lot of the doctors there were Japanese-American and the members of the board of directors were Japanese.

"Kuakini Hospital was funded by the Emperor of Japan to treat and care for Japanese immigrants, a lot of whom were retired plantation workers. It was built after a lot of their houses were accidentally destroyed in a fire that was started by the government to stop the spread of bubonic plague in Chinatown.

"During World War II Kuakini was taken over by the U.S. Army. It was the only hospital the Army ever officially *occupied* during the war."

Ultra-Emergency Surgery

The Other Dr. Delaney

"When I was working at Queens Hospital in Hawaii a guy came in with a ruptured aorta. His wife told me he was a retired general surgeon from Wisconsin and that he had an aortic aneurysm.

"You could tell his aorta had ruptured because his abdomen was really swollen.

"I put him in the floor of the outpatient clinic and cut him open, no gloves, no anesthetic, no nothing. There was so much blood I couldn't see very well, but I managed to clamp his aorta.

"I clamped it above his renal arteries. It was the best thing I could do for him. It saved his life, but because I'd put the clamp above the kidneys I destroyed his kidneys.

"He lived, but he had to be on dialysis the rest of his life."

Winters in Florida

Dr. Tucker

"In the winter the veterans hospitals in Florida filled up with former soldiers who lived most of the year as hobos and drunks up north, but who came down south when it got cold.

"A lot of them were Sterno drinkers. They called the drink *squeeze* because they made it by squeezing the alcohol out of the semi-solid mixture of candle wax and liquid that's canned and sold for a portable heat source. It's not meant for human consumption. It's what caterers use to keep chafing dishes warm.

"When these homeless guys would come in, many of them had lice. They'd be asked to disrobe and they'd be dipped in big vats like dogs in a flea bath. They'd have the guy climb into a tank, and they'd submerge him completely several times to remove the live organisms. Then they'd shower him down.

"Until you see things like this you might not realize how tough people are. They can make it through even the most terrible conditions. The truth is, with many illnesses, people will get better on their own.

"In medical school I was taught that most sick people would make it just fine without me. I've always remembered that.

"When I was first starting out I'd put my patients on the most innocuous stuff I could think of. I tried not to do anything that would hurt them.

"First do no harm—that's the key."

Good to Know
Moderation

"There's something to be said for moderation in life. We lose track of that in the overload of contradictory medical opinions spewing out of the modern media. We're not sure what's good and what's bad anymore.

"The simple truth is that moderation is the key to good health."

BECOMING A DOCTOR
Motives and Trajectories

Careers in radiology emerge from wildly varied contexts. They can be the final stage of a long struggle out of poverty, the continuation of a multi-generational family tradition, a crowning achievement following a doctorate in nuclear or biomedical engineering, or a change of direction subsequent to training in a different medical specialty.

Martial Arts to Medical Arts

Dr. Isaacs

"I'm Orthodox Jewish, the son of immigrants, and the first generation of my family to be born in America. Being in a concentration camp prevented my parents from getting the education they deserved, so I had little help in deciding what I was going to do with my life.

"My father worked eighty to a hundred hours a week from 1951 when he was forty years old, until 1999 when he was eighty-nine years old. He had to commute by train during all those years because he never learned to drive a car.

"After World War II, and for the rest of her life, my mother couldn't bear to be near authority figures because they reminded her of the camps.

"When I was a kid I submitted a story to *Reader's Digest* and it was published! I was a poster boy on the inside flap because my mother didn't learn English until 1948, and she learned the language by reading *Reader's Digest*.

"My mother had a huge vocabulary, but she never talked to anybody, so she taught me some incorrect pronunciations. She pronounced *pet peeve* as *pet PEEVEE*. She taught me to say *extravaganza* instead of *extravagance* and I pronounced *extravagance* as *extra-VAGONCE*.

"I got into a specialized science school and did well academically, but I didn't make my school basketball team, so I went out for judo. I was good at it. At the Jewish Welfare Board trials when I was a yellow belt, I used a maneuver on a black belt that made him look foolish. That made him angry and he gave me a severe injury to my left elbow.

"It was kinda dislocated, but everyone told me it was just a strain, so I didn't get seen. I had pinpoint pain in three or four areas, and within two weeks my left arm was fixed at nineteen degrees and immovable.

"My father worked nights and hardly ever saw me, but he insisted the Local 338 Retail Grocers Union have me evaluated. A month later I managed to get x-rayed, but they lost the images!

"When I finally got an evaluation it turned out that I had breaks in the radius, ulna, and humerus, as well as chips in the elbow joint. I couldn't use my left elbow. I couldn't extend my arm.

"I had orthopedic surgery and that was my introduction to American hospital care. The experience made me promise myself that I would never again be in a situation where I didn't know what was going on—either for me or for my family—so I decided to go to medical school.

"I wanted to be in a field that was helpful to society, to repay this country for letting my folks in, and I wanted do something that would give me a life I could be proud of.

"After medical school, when it came time to specialize, my friends went into radiology, so I decided to do it, too.

"It's a very broad field. Radiology has surgery, computers, patients and patient interaction—or, if you want to, you can stay in a dark room by yourself and read films.

"I didn't want to sit in a dark room by myself all day. I like patients. I like people. I like talking. So I engage with my colleagues. I see patients. I teach."

Your New Best Friend

Dr. Chapman

"There weren't many women in medical school when I went. That meant I had to endure some hazing, like being walked through the cadaver room while the bodies were still being prepared for the anatomy lab. They were hanging up, still leaking preservative fluid into drains in the floor.

"The men who led me through there hoped the sight would send me running home, but it didn't. It was horrible, but I pretended like it was nothing.

"Later I had to shut my eyes during some of the medical slide shows because they made me sick. But I eventually got over it.

"During my internship I used to hide in the bathroom and cry after an emergency was over. We weren't supposed to do that. But just as I'd gotten over my squeamishness, I gradually learned to stay calm during an emergency and tell people what to do."

"Nobody starts out ready to do the complicated kinds of surgical procedures an interventional radiologist does. You're conditioned to it gradually over many years. The conditioning starts on the first day of medical school when there are a hundred students standing in a room with fifty cadavers covered with shrouds.

"They tell you to go stand by a table. Then they tell you to pull the shroud.

"It's not the easiest thing in the world to do, but you do it and you stand there next to the dead body.

"Then they tell you, *This is your friend for the next year.*

"One guy in my class walked out the first day right after the shroud removal and he never came back. Some people get wobbly, some even faint, but they stay with it. They overcome their emotional reactions.

"It *is* shocking. But I grew up hunting and fishing and cleaning game, so I could cope. A lot of people want to leave on that first day when they have to work with a dead person, but they don't. You feel squeamish, your knees get weak a time or two, but after that you're all right.

"A lot of medical students get light-headed when they assist in surgery for the first time, or the first time they see an autopsy. One of my classmates got sick every single time he saw blood and he couldn't overcome it, so he became a psychiatrist.

"Some aspects of radiology involve minimally invasive surgery. Interventional radiologists pioneered the procedures guided with fluoroscopy, ultrasound, CT, or MRI that are commonly done these days so patients don't have to undergo major surgery.

"The ability to do surgery requires a special personality. Surgeons are the kind of people who are most at home and peaceful when they're operating. Rather than upsetting them, performing surgery calms them down.

"For me, I've found that the most peaceful times are when I'm doing complicated procedures, like surgery. The hard times are when you're *not* doing surgery.

"The hard times are when you're outside of the surgical suite dealing with the business types, the administrators and bureaucrats who know nothing about caring for a patient but who've gotten in charge of medicine."

Making the Decision

Dr. Powell

"It was easy for me to decide to become a doctor.

"My dad was a family practice doctor. I was born when he was fifty-five years old.

"Through his work he created a huge extended network in the town where we lived. I was always meeting people and learning that my dad had delivered them and taken care of them. I wanted to continue his legacy.

"But the world changed a lot between my dad's generation and mine. The way family practice doctors worked has been crippled by the changes in the healthcare system.

"The general practitioner used to be the doctor for the whole family, handling everything from birth through to the end of life. He was like a member of your family. Now he's been relegated to a referral service, a gateway to specialists.

"By the time I got out of medical school I realized it wasn't going to be possible for me to have the same sort of life as my father, where he'd be called out in the middle of the night and have to perform an emergency appendectomy or a C-section.

"Now it takes so long to make a doctor, from the time you enter college until you finish your residency, the whole landscape of medicine can change, everything from the technology to politics and the economics of practice.

"Newly graduating FPs have huge student loans. They have the same amount of debt that the specialists have, and yet the primary care patients want a quick fix. They want to be able to call the doctor's office and leave a phone message telling him to write them antibiotics whenever they want them, without allowing him to see them.

"That's not good medical practice. Sick patients should be seen by a doctor for a proper diagnosis. They shouldn't instruct the physician on the basis of an amateur self-diagnosis.

"In general practice after the end of World War II, in the earliest days of antibiotics, you'd say, 'I've got a sore throat,' and you'd get a shot of penicillin.

"We've gradually become aware of the downside of overusing antibiotics. Now doctors will say, 'Let's do a culture and be sure what you need.' But patients can't or don't want to pay for an exam or for any tests and they get mad.

"It's sad, but that's the way it is now, so I went into radiology instead."

34

* * *

Dr. McDowell

"I always wanted to be a doctor, ever since I was a little boy.

"My mother was a midwife in a small town in Georgia. She was the matriarch of the town. She took care of everyone, including indigents. She took care of *everything*.

"Anybody who had a problem, medical or otherwise, they came to her. And she helped them. I wanted to help people like she did."

* * *

Dr. Morrison

"Both of my parents are physicians, and both of my brothers are physicians. My dad and my older brothers are neurosurgeons, so that's the first profession I was exposed to.

"My dad says when I was five years old, I asked him, 'Hey Dad, what do you call the guys who read x-rays?' He said, 'Radiologists.' And I said, 'That's what I want to be.'

"I used to go watch my dad at the hospital. I watched him read x-rays and look at CT scans. My choosing neuroradiology seemed like a revelation when it finally happened, but a strong foundation had been laid by my father and brothers."

* * *

Dr. Lawrence

"Between college and medical school I worked as a biomedical engineer. I like academics and the technical aspects of things. I love solving puzzles and logic problems.

"Midway through medical school I realized I especially enjoyed figuring out diagnoses. In radiology I can do that and also use technology to do it."

"When I first moved to Memphis to work as a radiologist, I didn't know my new colleagues so I made an effort to reach out to them. For example, when you're consulting with a physician about an MRI, there are a lot of images to discuss.

"So, instead of saying over the phone, 'Look at the fourth image on the bottom left,' I'd ask, 'Where are you?' Then I'd go over to their hospital and review the images with them face-to-face.

"After I did that for a while physicians started coming by my department before I even had the chance to call them. That's the kind of interaction I really enjoy.

"Neuroradiology a very large and complex subfield of radiology. It concerns MRI and CT scans of the brain, spine, neck, face, and orbits. I get to review cases with the primary treating physicians, with surgeons, ophthalmologists, otolaryngologists, neurosurgeons, orthopedists, and infectious disease specialists.

"It's a good fit for me."

* * *

Dr. Hawkins

"I like being challenged academically. I like to push the limits of where I can go. I also like to see the direct impact of what I do. In engineering it takes many, many years to see an impact. In medicine there is more satisfaction seeing results in your day-to-day work.

"Working with radiation and nuclear materials can keep you away from people if you let it, but I'm more of a people person. I'm not happy alone at a desk.

"I wanted more patient contact and direct hands-on caring for patients, so I sought out a subspecialty where I could have it: radiation oncology.

"Oncology has a lot of tough cases. Not everyone is able to cope with that.

"I've noticed that some people are able to find happiness whatever life brings them. I was always an optimist, even as a nuclear engineer.

"I'm still that way."

* * *

Dr. Weiss

"I wanted to be a family practitioner when I started medical school, but when I was about to graduate I changed my plan and decided to go into radiology because of something I experienced in my own family.

"My grandmother had a massive stroke, a huge stroke. Overnight she went from being a vibrant lady to someone who couldn't communicate well and who needed a lot of help.

"I could see the sadness in her face at no longer being able to share her thoughts and ideas and interests with her family. That's why I chose radiology.

"I wanted to be an interventional radiologist so I could remove clots and mitigate or reverse strokes. My grandmother's stroke changed my whole life trajectory.

"I did all the schooling and then studied for an additional year. But during the time it took me to go through the training, the interventional subspecialty changed significantly.

"Various other types of specialists began to perform the minimally invasive vascular surgical procedures radiologists had pioneered.

"I was doing a fellowship in the best radiology program in the country. While I was there the number of angiogram procedures dropped fifty percent. That's a *lot*. Since then it's dropped even more.

"I had planned to work in middle Tennessee, but just before I was ready to start, the hospital in Nashville fired the radiology group because the cardiology group wanted to read the heart images.

"There's a constant land grab going on among the specialties for patients and procedures. Everything is changing all the time—the technology as well as who reads the images."

"PRACTICING" MEDICINE
The ER and General Practice

Before one is allowed to revel in the monastic peace and quiet of a reading room, they must survive a long journey through chaotic and dangerous territory as a medical student, intern, resident, and perhaps even a fellow.

Doctors whose careers were interrupted by war sometimes did stints in general practice while awaiting the start of their specialty training. But no matter where the earliest years of practice were spent, they were inevitably punctuated by a variety of traumatic medical experiences that steered careers either toward or away from certain types of patient contact.

Assisting with childbirth, surgery, autopsies, or the emergency room tended to make the strongest impressions on young doctors. These environments provoked crises wherein all one's previous training might be thrown out the window in an effort to simply survive.

Sometimes even the most fundamental principle taught in medical school, Primum non nocere, *or* First do no harm, *would be set aside, at least for a couple of minutes.*

First Do No Harm

Dr. Adams

"I trained at Jackson Memorial, the big charity hospital in Miami. One night when I was working in the ER the police brought a prisoner in.

"The patient was a real sociopath who'd just killed two policemen in a fierce gun battle.

"He'd been shot several times and had serious wounds to his chest and abdomen. He was hurt pretty bad, but he was going to be okay if he had time to heal. In the meantime his breathing had to be supported by a ventilator.

"The chief resident in thoracic surgery was taking a look at the gunshot wounds and the exam was unavoidably painful on account of the guy's injuries.

"The prisoner was obviously a very angry person and he wasn't enjoying what the resident was doing.

"He couldn't talk because he had a ventilator tube down his throat, but he made hand motions to indicate that he wanted to write something.

"The nurse brought him a pencil and paper, and he scrawled, *When I get out of this bed I'm gonna kill you*, and held it up toward the doctor.

"The chest surgeon read the note and then reached over and unplugged the ventilator.

"We stood there beside the guy's bed and waited.

"After a couple of minutes his breathing started to fail. Clearly he was going to smother to death in short order, but none of us moved or said anything.

"The cop killer snatched up his pencil and paper again. This time he scribbled, *I'm sorry, I take it back*, and held it up so the surgeon could read it.

"The doctor plugged the ventilator back in.

"After that the guy's attitude improved significantly. We treated his injuries, he got well, and then he went to prison for the rest of his life."

Hospitals Southern Style:
Tornados, Hurricanes, Floods, and the
Walking Dead

Dr. Grant

"You can't imagine what it was like to work in one of the huge charity hospitals in the South. Tens of thousands of young doctors were trained at the iconic institutions in Miami, New Orleans, Atlanta, or Memphis.

"The kinds of things went on inside these hospitals are unimaginable today. For one, they used to be segregated. There were Colored and White emergency rooms. The doctors went back and forth from one to the other.

"There were Colored and White drinking fountains, restrooms, and wards, too. There had to be two of everything, sometimes in separate wings, and sometimes on separate floors. That's why they called Grady Memorial in Atlanta *The Gradys*. Some people still call it that.

"Each of these hospitals has had some sort of catastrophe and for the most part they've withstood them. Grady was damaged by a tornado and is still going strong, but I've heard nowadays it's also used as a filming location for *The Walking Dead*.

"Jackson Memorial in Miami was devastated by the Great Miami Hurricane in the '20s. All their patients all had to be carried down the stairs to protect them from the glass and whatnot that was getting blown around.

"There wasn't any electricity so they did surgery by kerosene lantern while standing in the floodwater. Now Jackson is the largest hospital in the country. It has more than 1,700 beds. Grady is Number 7.

"Charity Hospital, L'Hospital des Pauvres de la Charité, in New Orleans was started with money from a Frenchman's estate in the early 1700s. *Big Charity*, as it was called, used to have the busiest ER in the USA. It survived for nearly 300 years until 2005 when Hurricane Katrina finally got the better of it.

"New Orleans and Miami are more cosmopolitan environments than the other places on account of centuries of French and Spanish immigration, then Cuban and Haitian, and others. You see a lot of things in major port cities that you won't see elsewhere because of the maritime influence.

"John Gaston in Memphis, although it's technically the northernmost of the legendary southern hospitals, operated as the most stereotypically *southern*

41

in culture. That's because Memphis functions more like the capitol of Mississippi than as a part of Tennessee.

"*The Gaston*, had a lot of nicknames—the JG, the Gas House, or the Gast-AWN pronounced with an exaggerated French accent. This was where University of Tennessee medical students were exposed to indigent patients and trained in the medical practices of the Deep South.

"It was finally torn down in 1990."

Bed & Breakfast

Dr. Abrams

"When I was training at Jackson in Miami there were 1,300 beds in an un-air-conditioned hospital. One of my strongest memories of that place is of going into a ward at five in the morning to draw blood from an old gentleman.

"I found my patient in bed holding a fork in one hand and a shoe in the other. He was whacking at bugs with his slipper—trying to fend off an army of roaches—so he could eat his breakfast.

"I sat down on the edge of his bed and used his other shoe to help him kill them so he could have his meal.

"In Florida the roaches are called *palmetto bugs*. They're huge, they can fly, and they're real hard to get rid of.

"They don't tell you about situations like this in medical school.

"Jackson is even bigger now, the biggest hospital in the whole country. Thank goodness they got air-conditioning."

***

"They Don't Call It the Emergency Room for Nothing"

***

Cosmetic Surgery

Dr. Leighton

"Although we don't get much credit for it, medical work can get downright dangerous.

"During my early training we'd be trying to suture knife wounds in the emergency room with both combatants at the same hospital at the same time, still screaming at each other, punching and flailing away through the curtains between the treatment areas.

"I've been in more than one hospital when there was live gunfire going on.

"The guys we were sewing up wanted big scars that would make them look tough. They'd ask us to stitch their lacerations so they'd look bad. 'Use your thickest thread,' they'd say."

Lend Me Your Ear

"Fridays and Saturdays are always the busiest nights in the emergency room. It's when the drunks come in.

"Some of them come in on their own, others are brought in by the police.

"This situation was predictable enough and problematic enough that the hospitals always hired their own security guys to work on Fridays and Saturdays.

"On one of these nights a woman came in carrying part of her ear. Her boyfriend had bitten it off.

"I sewed it back on as best I could.

"I'd never sewed an ear on before.

"I've never done it since, either."

Head Case

"One night when I was a resident at *The Gaston* in Memphis, Sven the intern was sewing someone up in the ER. 'I sewed these two lacerations,' he told me, pointing at them. 'This one is from the policeman, and this one is from me.'

"Sven had been provoked into hitting his patient in the head with a needleholder during the operation. I could understand how these things might happen, so I didn't criticize him. He'd done a nice job sewing up both of the cuts."

Not a White Collar Profession

Dr. Vandenberg

"A teenager hopped up on drugs came in to the ER and was shoving a nurse around.

"We needed to separate him from the nurse, so I came up behind him and grabbed him in a chokehold. Security was called but it took a while for them to arrive.

"During my struggle with him I got a couple of teeth knocked out and a rib broken.

"When the police got there it took several of them to get control of the guy.

"Medicine isn't a white collar job.

"I had to get crowns on my two front teeth and that broken rib really hurt. Ever since then I've always felt sorry for people who get multiple rib fractures. That's gotta be terribly painful. I had just the one and it was bad enough."

Code Red

Dr. Norman

"Crazy things happen in the ER all the time, but unfortunately you can never predict when it will happen, what it will be, or who it will happen to.

"One time I was running down the hall, responding to a call for help on a cardiac arrest. I took a shortcut through the ER waiting area.

"A guy with an upper respiratory infection who must've been waiting a long time to be seen suddenly reached the end of his patience. He saw me coming in my white coat and jumped up as I ran past him.

"With no warning at all, he punched me hard in the face and broke my nose. He didn't seem to care that someone's heart had stopped and that I was the doctor who was supposed to get it started again.

"My nose was bleeding heavily and it hurt like the dickens, but I had a job to do and I didn't have time to get into a fistfight with the guy or explain where I was going and why.

"I hardly slowed down. I grabbed my nose and pinched it tight to try to stop the bleeding, and kept right on running. All I could think was, *How am I gonna run the code when I'm bleeding like this?*"

Hole in the Head

Dr. Shaw

"I was on duty in the emergency room and went into a little curtained area to see my next patient. A guy was sitting up on the gurney.

"'What's the problem?' I asked.

"'I got shot in the head,' he said.

"I examined him and, sure enough, the man had a neat little hole in his forehead. He'd been lucky and the bullet hadn't penetrated very far. It had gone around the outside of his skull, just underneath the skin. You could feel it beneath the scalp on the backside of his head.

"In the ER you see the full range of humanity. You get the guy who'd never come in on his own no matter what the problem was. This type only shows up when they're nearly dead and are carried in unconscious by EMTs or Good Samaritans.

"And you see another type of person who comes in way too often. They show up every week with all sorts of complaints and always leave with no diagnosis.

"People vary enormously in their response to pain."

Just a Flesh Wound

Dr. Carter

"An old gentleman came in to emergency room.

"'What's goin on?' I asked him.

"'I got the miseries,' he said. 'I can't get around very good. I feel real bad all over.'

"I examined him and noticed an injury on his chest. 'What's this?' I asked.

"'I got shot,' he said.

"Turns out he'd been shot in the chest a week earlier.

"'I heard a gunshot,' he said, 'and felt a pain in my chest. But it wasn't too bad, so I thought the bullet had just grazed me. I went home and laid down, but it got worse. Then, for a few days after that, I was too sick to come in.'

"The man had a pneumothorax. Half his chest was filled with blood and the pressure of it had collapsed one of his lungs. That is a very serious and extremely painful condition, but the guy's vital signs weren't too bad.

"He didn't understand what had happened to him and was nonchalant about the whole thing.

"He had to have immediate thoracic surgery, of course."

Appalachian Anatomy Lesson

Dr. Eaton

"A doctor from Boston who was trained in chest medicine accepted a pulmonary position in Miami that was going to start in a couple of months. He decided to find some temporary work to fill the gap until his permanent job started.

"He came to Newport, Tennessee having no idea what he was getting himself into. He wore little wire-rimmed glasses and had a ponytail. This didn't fit in well with the local folks.

"One day I heard a big man come stomping down the hall, hollering, 'That little hippy doctor. I'm gonna yank his arms off and use 'em to whup him.'

"Apparently the guy didn't find the doctor because he left without any further outbursts. When he was gone, the Boston doctor reappeared from where he'd been hiding, and asked me, 'Jesus Christ, what's a *goozle?*'

"'It's your throat,' I said.

"'Oh! How do you know that?'

"'I'm from East Tennessee!' I said.

"Then he confessed that the man's chief complaint was that he had *a sore goozle*. The Boston doctor hadn't understood what the big guy, a logger by trade, meant, so he'd tried to check him for a hernia. That's when things got ugly."

Stereotypes

Dr. Davi

"My family moved from Pakistan to the U.S. when I was seven years old.

"I grew up in New York City, in Brooklyn, and went to a diverse multi-cultural middle school. Over time I developed rapid speech with a distinct northern accent.

"Several years later my family relocated to a small town in North Carolina. We were so different from the locals that people would drive by our house just to see what a brown person looked like.

"They had no idea where Pakistan was. It took nearly a year for me to adjust to that new environment, slow my speech and alter my accent, so I could fit in.

"Then, after college and medical school in Tennessee, I moved back up north for specialty training at the Cleveland Clinic. At first I had a perceptible southern accent, but gradually my accent adjusted itself again to blend in to the north.

"When my training was finished I moved back down south to Georgia. So, for most of my life I've been in a continuous process of adapting to different cultures, but sometimes I still get baffled.

"The biggest double take I've ever experienced was during an encounter with another Pakistani Muslim. He was a colleague at the Cleveland Clinic.

"He had the heaviest southern accent you could imagine and he spoke in a perfect southern redneck vernacular.

"He'd been born in Pakistan, grown up in Texas, and gone to school at Vanderbilt. Part of the profound shock I experienced when meeting him was caused by the fact that he wasn't from just *anywhere* in Pakistan. He was from the northwest frontier. That's the most rural location imaginable, and it's an extremely anti-West area.

"It was startling to encounter this fellow and realize how shocked I was because of my own cultural preconceptions. That guy destroys every stereotype you can imagine."

Hat Trick

Dr. Samuels

"When I came home from the military, before I became a radiologist, I worked for a while as a general practitioner in Cocke County, Tennessee.

"The area around Newport and the little town of Del Rio is an unusual place. The culture there is highly distinctive along the lines of the most notorious Appalachian stereotypes.

"I grew up in east Tennessee, but even then I had some things to learn about the more obscure local traditions.

"There was no county hospital, so two local doctors established the Valentine-Schultz Hospital. My office was right across the street from it.

"Shortly after I started work there, a rough fellow came to my office and demanded forty Percocets. I wasn't sure what to do so I fobbed him off temporarily and went to one of the local doctors to ask for advice.

"This particular physician had the benefit of two years of OB/GYN training and was the mayor more than once. He was very politically connected, knew everyone, and smoked a cigar all the time.

"When I asked him how I should handle this fellow's demand for narcotics, he said, 'I can tell you this. He's kilt seven men. You can do whatever you want to. But personally, I give him any damn thing he wants.'

"I thought about it and decided to compromise. I gave him twenty Percocets. You want to have the worst sociopath in the area on your side, then everyone else will leave you alone."

"I'd go up into the mountains to assist with childbirth in places where they relied mostly on midwives. I learned to deliver babies under the sheets with the husband standing over me holding a gun.

"On one call, a midwife was already there when I arrived. The woman's husband was standing in the middle of the room cradling a shotgun. He didn't say it straight out, but the implication was clear that if things didn't go well, he was gonna use the gun on us.

"There was a problem during the delivery. The woman clamped down on the placenta. When this happens all you can do is gently pull on the cord until the placenta comes loose. I carefully tugged and tugged, but it wasn't coming loose.

"The woman was bleeding and the midwife got worried that the husband was gonna kill us. 'If you'll put the old man's hat under the bed,' she whispered, 'it'll turn loose.'

"Then let's git that hat," I said.

"We got the husband's hat and put it under the bed and ten seconds later, out came the placenta. Everything turned out fine. Both the mother and the baby did well.

"That was a good lesson for me. Ever since then I've always said, *You can't discount anything in this medicine game.*"

Another young radiologist-to-be also faced a rough delivery involving a retained placenta while working a stint in general practice.

Up to My Elbows In ...

Dr. Lowell

"One evening my wife and I were preparing to go out to dinner when I got a call from a patient who was in labor and ready to deliver.

"My wife said she'd like to go along so she could see me deliver a baby. We went to the local hospital and my wife got all gowned up and stood back out of the way, in a place where she could watch.

"Unfortunately, the delivery didn't go well. Things got complicated and then they got dangerous. The mother had a retained placenta.

"I knew this was going to shake my wife up, but the situation was beyond anyone's control. All I could do was try to deal with it the best I could.

"I got my hand *way* up inside the mother, but you don't just yank on the cord and rip everything out. You mustn't do that, in fact. You have to be *really* careful or you can cause the mother to bleed to death.

"You use one hand to work the placenta loose gradually. Then you can deliver baby and, after that, the placenta.

"I had my arm up inside the mother all the way to my elbow and was carefully working the placenta loose. I glanced over at my wife and saw that she was wobbling.

"The mother and baby did fine, but my wife was pretty traumatized. After that, she never requested to see another procedure.

"I was sorry she'd had such a rough experience that first time. I thought it was gonna be a routine delivery or I wouldn't have let her watch.

"You just never know what's gonna happen. You show up and you do your best, but an awful lot of aspects of medicine are out of everyone's control."

Appalachian Medicine

Dr. Phelps

"When I arrived in Hancock County the treatment for chicken pox was to fly chickens over the afflicted individual. If a kid was sick, they'd put him in front of the chicken coop and someone would shoo the chickens in such a way that they'd take flight up and over the child's head.

"That was the locally accepted cure.

"If you had *the itch* they'd cover you with sulfur and molasses and send you over to the other side of the pasture to get well because you stank.

"I've never been clear on exactly what *the itch* was.

"Patients would say, 'I've got a misery.'

"'What kinda misery?' I'd ask.

"'I got a creepin misery. It creeps up my leg and walks over here,' and they'd point to where it hurt.

"People would wear asafetida bags for various problems and they'd rub Vicks on their chests to treat cases of pneumonia.

"They'd *grease* babies by rubbing them all over with lard or bacon grease. In Memphis the mothers would do this especially if their baby had a fever.

"Being a doctor in places like that can be especially frustrating because a lot of your patients don't understand much about modern medicine. You have to take the time to talk to them and explain things. But even then, sometimes they'll complain with comments like, 'My daddy had a heart attack and you didn't even give him a shot of penicillin!'"

"I had an unforgettable couple as patients. Their names were Ben and Stella.

"Ben came in with a red bandana wrapped around his head. He'd tied it and twisted tight with a stick. When I asked him about it he said it was to ward off headaches.

"I asked him if he had a headache and he said he didn't. His treatment was obviously effective, so I didn't dispute it.

"Stella wore an old pair of glasses with one lens so fogged up you couldn't even see through it. Ben did most of the talking for them both.

"I asked Ben what the problem was that had brought him in to see me and he said he'd started having trouble with arthritis. He said, 'I taken me eight doses of Sure-Gel.'

"I waited for him to say more, but he didn't add anything, so I realized that pectin must be his remedy for arthritis. 'How's your arthritis?' I asked.

"'My arthritis is pretty good,' he said, 'but my bowels hadn't moved in three weeks.'

"When the pectin gets warm it's supposed to melt, but apparently Ben's eight doses weren't melting, so I sent him on to a radiologist for a clean out.

"Radiologists have a substance they use in their work that will guarantee a bowel movement.

"The radiologist who supervised Ben's enema told me later, 'That was the dangdest looking stuff I ever saw.'"

"When I asked them where they lived, Stella said, 'Back where the Lord lost his boots.'

"Their children were so filthy they had dirt embedded in their skin. 'Mam,' I said, 'you've gotta give these children a bath.'

"'We ain't got narry an bathtub,' Stella said.

"'You've got Lye soap and creek,' I said. This solution was apparently a revelation to her.

"'By God,' she said, with great enthusiasm, 'come spring we'll *all* just take us a bath!'

"People might think these sorts of situations are just stereotypes, that they don't really exist anywhere in the real world, but they do. Stereotypes don't emerge from thin air. They come from somewhere.

"These are good people. They aren't stupid. It's just that they've grown up with different educational opportunities and they've had different life experiences from the mainstream.

"The fact that they resemble unflattering stereotypes in other parts of the country, or because their culture is unfamiliar to most people, doesn't mean their lives have any less value than someone who happened to be born a few hundred miles away."

Road Scholars

Dr. Coleman

"I did quite a bit of obstetrical work in rural east Tennessee. I delivered thirty babies in my last month of general practice. The biggest OB doctor in Knoxville delivered only twenty-eight!

"It was an amazing experience. Men would show up at my office in an old pickup truck and their wives would be lying in the back with a baby partially sticking out of them.

"All you could see would be two little purple feet, telling you the baby was anoxic.

"I'd give the woman ether to relax her uterus, then reach up inside her and grab the baby's jawbone and pull the kid out.

"After such a tough start in life those kids might not grow up to be Rhodes Scholars, but they probably wouldn't have the opportunities for that anyway."

"The Grand Wizard of the local snake handler church was one of my patients.

"He came to see me several times for various non-snake-related medical problems. I knew he secretly milked the snakes before he or his parishioners handled them.

"Ten years after I left town one of his snakes bit him and killed him when he was milking it. Snakes don't always inject when they bite, but if they haven't been milked recently and they bite you, and decide to really let you have it, you can certainly die."

Conflicting Priorities

Dr. Coleman

"One day I was in the office putting in an intrauterine device—a Lippes Loop. My patient was in the stirrups, and I had the speculum in. I'd just installed the IUD and suddenly there was a big commotion at the back door of my office.

"I could hear someone talking excitedly to Marie, my nurse.

"'It's an emergency,' they said. Two people had been brought in to the ER with multiple gunshot wounds.

"The small local hospital was just across the road from my office, so I jumped up and ran over to the ER. I didn't really mean to, but I abandoned the lady in the stirrups, and then in the chaos of tending to the gunshot wounds, I completely forgot about her.

"Hours later, when I finally returned to my office, I discovered that my patient had waited a long time for me to come back, and then, when I didn't, she'd gotten herself out of the stirrups and changed back into her street clothes. Nobody was in the room with her to tell her any different so she kept the speculum in.

"When she came out of the room, she called out to my nurse, 'Marie, I heared tell these thangs was uncomfortable, but this is *ridiculous*!'

"Marie took her back into the examining room and discovered that the woman had somehow managed to put her underwear on over the stainless steel instrument. I can't imagine how she was able to do this, because although half the instrument was inside her, the large metal handle grips and an adjustable length of steel that you use to lock the device open were still protruding from her body.

"Marie removed the instrument and sent my patient on her way in considerably less discomfort."

"The emergency at the hospital was the result of an argument over a boundary line. A father and son were digging a posthole for a fence and got into a dispute with their neighbor.

"The disagreement concerned a matter of only a few feet, but the people of East Tennessee are different. It's a violent place. One of the guys believed his neighbor was encroaching on his property, so he shot the daddy and the son five times apiece.

"The son died before he reached the hospital.

"I didn't have a lot of blood available for a transfusion, so I stabilized the daddy as well as I could, then put him in an ambulance and sent him on to Knoxville. He survived.

"When the sheriff went to get the killer, he found the man sitting in his living room calmly watching soap operas. He'd already dismissed the events from his mind."

"In West Tennessee things are a little different. Memphis shooters aim at each other's genitals. They generally hit a leg.

"When I became a radiologist I did a lot of angiography at John Gaston Hospital. The emergency room at *The Gaston* was called *The Friday Night Knife & Gun Club.*

"The x-ray techs got extra money to work at the hospital on Friday and Saturdays nights because it was such a wild place. We called the bonuses *combat pay.*

"Women aren't as prone to using guns. Their approach is more subtle. I had a female patient who came in with the complaint of, 'I dropped my roses three times this week.'

"I understood this was her way of saying that she'd experienced three episodes of vaginal bleeding during the previous week. So, I did a pelvic exam.

"I discovered a razor blade in her vagina. 'You've got a razor blade in you,' I said. 'How'd that get in there?'

"'I put it in there for Mr. John,' she said, 'because he just push me down and takes it.'

"I told her she shouldn't continue this particular strategy to punish Mr. John because the razor blade was cutting her inside and that was what was causing the bleeding.

"I removed the razor blade and she promised not to put another one inside herself, but I could tell she was disappointed that Mr. John hadn't gotten what he deserved."

Lights On, Nobody Home

Dr. Miller

"Many years ago when I was in general practice I used to make house calls.

"Back then the biggest problem you faced was finding the right house.

"It wasn't until relatively recently that houses in rural areas got individual numerical addresses. Some areas still don't have them. When I was making house calls all people had was a postal address like *Jimmy Jones, Rural Route 4, Tazewell, Tennessee.*

"It could be nearly impossible to find a particular house if you hadn't been raised in the area. Patients would say, 'The porch light'll be on,' and you'd drive out looking for the place, but the porch lights would be on at every house on the road.

"Or you might have the opposite problem and that's just as bad. This was in the days before cell phones or GPS.

"Late one night I was called out to see a man whose wife gave me some vague directions and then added the usual, 'We'll turn the porch light on.'

"I drove up and down the road for an hour without seeing a single light on. Finally I got exasperated and went home.

"I called my patient to apologize for being unable to locate his house. His wife said, 'Oh he got to feelin' better, so we turned the light off.'"

Stress Test

Dr. Annenberg

"One time I treated a sick kid and his mother brought him back in an hour later, all twisted and turned like the worst case of muscular dystrophy you'd ever seen.

"I was baffled, and horrified. I'd given the child a commonly used broad-spectrum antibiotic and a suppository for nausea. I wondered, *What have I had done to this little boy?*

"He was terrible looking. Thank heavens he was back to normal in a few hours, about the same amount of time it took me to research what had happened. This was the pre-Google era.

"I'd given the boy a Compazine suppository for nausea. It can cause a side-effect of dystonia in some children. I always gave children a different medicine for nausea after that.

"You learn as you go. Some lessons are more distressing than others."

"When you do surgery you can get into some tough situations, especially if you're working in a remote area without a lot of resources. Things can suddenly become precarious, and you have to find a way to deal with the challenges.

"Once I delivered a baby by C-section in a small rural hospital. The woman had a uterine abnormality and she started to hemorrhage.

"In cases like hers it was recommended to deliver the baby and do a hysterectomy immediately afterwards. I would've done that but I didn't have enough blood to transfuse her, and I had no fibrinogen, a clotting factor, to give her.

"That meant I *couldn't* do a hysterectomy. So I did the best I could, and she and the baby lived.

"In situations like that you feel an extreme urgency. You know you've gotta do something fast. You've gotta be quick.

"When you're doing a high-risk procedure you get tense.

"Interventional radiology is a stressful profession. If you really care about what you're doing, if you care about your patient, there's a lot of pressure and a lot of stress.

"Added to this stress is the fact that now doctors are expected to be a hundred percent right a hundred percent of the time. This is tough, because in reality *nobody* is right all the time.

"I saved a guy's life once and he sued me. I got sued just that one time in my whole career. I won the case in court, but it was a miserable process. It took three years.

"Being sued by the guy was even more upsetting because he had no lingering disability or problems from what I'd done.

"You work extremely long hours, you do the very best you can—knowing that if *anything* goes wrong, you'll be attacked and scrutinized and harried for *years*. Lawyers will try to turn the doctors against each other, to see if they can find someone to scapegoat.

"It is an unfair situation especially when you consider that the reason you're seeing the person in the first place is because something bad has *already* happened to them. Before they came through the hospital door they were having a problem!

"This is a difficult aspect of medicine. You hear about it but you hope you'll never have to face it yourself. This is a part of medical practice that causes people to burn out or stress out."

THE DARK LORDS
Long Hours

The working conditions of some radiologist are extremely rarified. They are swathed in a hushed twilight cocoon, reading images with their backs to a surging ocean of technicians whose numbers are so vast I was reminded of scenes from the court of a pharaoh or of an Indian viceroy where the sole occupation of some of the silent and devoted attendants might be to wield a fly swatter or waft a fan over their master.

It was the polar opposite of the world I grew up in.

I was the child of a first-responder who was sometimes the only doctor for miles. My father had no backup and no fancy machines. He was often helped by a family member or a nurse, but my father did nearly everything that had to be done with his own hands.

Few radiologists work like that. They aren't the first stop for a sick or injured person, indeed, in some of the subspecialties they rarely clap eyes on an actual patient. Their interaction might be confined to examining static black and white images on a two-dimensional surface like a computer monitor. In that environment there's no screaming or cursing, no flailing legs or clutching hands, no tears, no bleeding, no urine, no vomit.

But before anyone can get to the pristine privacy of the reading room a radiologist has to undergo a lot of training in far less exalted circumstances.

Welcome to My World

Dr. Baker

"When you see a radiologist at work, you have no idea what it took for that guy to get where he is. His previous life may have been very different from where he ended up.

"A lot of us come from impoverished backgrounds or immigrant parents. We go through years, decades, dealing with a significant lack of sleep.

"Working in a hospital can be rough, especially in the emergency room. You get screamed at, punched. Our lives are threatened. You're present during knife fights and shootouts.

"Soldiers, policemen, boxers, football players—they understood that physical altercations would be a part of their jobs. I guess bartenders and drug dealers know it, too.

"But doctors and nurses and pharmacists? Most of us didn't realize we were signing up for this kind of thing.

"Our training is very academic. Then suddenly, when you get out of the classroom, you're greeted by the chaos of an urban hospital. It's quite a rude shock!

"You start at 5:00 a.m. and work all day and all night. You might work through the next day, too. Then you get a night off. You rotate through weekends, holidays, everything—working 90 to 120 hours a week.

"It's good to work really hard, to toughen up and learn to hold your concentration. But you shouldn't have to do it for *years*. Having to live like that changes you as a person.

"A lot of people go through those years and come out with a different personality than they had going in. They're overworked to the point where they lose the human side they used to have.

"They become unable to access the warmth they need to interact with their patients. Their attention gets turned inward, toward themselves and their concerns about how they're gonna survive this.

"There used to be so few doctors you might need to work three or four days straight, but this isn't necessary any more. That was the old system. It was hard to get away from it, but we have more people now.

"In my whole career I have *never* worked a forty-hour week. Most radiologists work sixty at least.

"For most of my career, when you'd read out all the images on your shift you weren't finished. You still had to correct all the transcription. Your

66

dictation is a legal document, so it has to be carefully done. It could take two hours at the end of each day to review it all.

"Sometimes the transcription would be so poor you couldn't recognize anything you'd said. It could be so bad you'd have to retrieve the image and read it all over again. Other times you wouldn't even be able to figure out which image you were talking about!"

Stretching Out

Dr. Klein

"There was a motel across the street from Jackson Memorial, the big charity hospital in Miami. The hospital bought it and converted it into sleeping quarters for people who were on call.

"I guess it seemed like a good idea at the time, but in reality nobody ever went there because the hospital was in a dangerous part of town and you were highly likely to get mugged before you could get inside your room.

"So, instead of risking getting robbed, whenever I needed ten minutes of *zzzs* I'd go to the place where the stretchers were stored. They were kept under some shelves that were stacked with blankets.

"When I was lying down, my feet were the only parts of me that you could see sticking out. The nurses knew where I was, though, so when they needed me they'd come pinch my toes to wake me up.

"Jackson was a great place to train. You saw everything that could possibly go wrong. It was a mecca of pathology. You saw all the diseases and learned by volume."

"I was up practically every night in the early days. It was before any of the hospitals had ER doctors. Now when I look back on it, I don't know how I did it, but at the time you just did what you had to do.

"Frequently I'd have to get up in the middle of the night, get dressed, and make a trip in to the hospital, sometimes more than once during a single night.

"One evening my wife asked me, 'Do you know how long it's been since you've been home for dinner?'

"'I have no idea!' I said. 'All I know is whether it's daylight or dark.'

"I could get by on very little sleep. I just did it. I had no choice. Now they have four guys doing what I was doing."

"We've all encountered doctors who've become notorious for behaving poorly at work. Nowadays there aren't quite as many of them who act out as there used to be.

"Part of the problem is the way we train doctors. You work so hard getting into and through medical school—and then you still have to survive an internship and a residency and maybe a fellowship. People have no idea how grueling it is.

"You might be on call every other night for *years*, and that can cause personality problems. You can see this develop in some specialties more than

68

others. Some physicians become really difficult to deal with. They get abusive—to staff, nurses, everyone. They complain about everything.

"They're ridiculous, but don't seem to realize it. I saw one guy rip a chart apart and throw it on the floor and jump up and down on it. You think of all the training that man had. And there he is, leaping up and down on torn pieces of paper in the middle of the hospital.

"When I was a resident I'd be sent to retrieve films for other doctors. If the request was being made by one of these unpleasant guys, the radiology department would suddenly appear to be empty. It would look like *no one* was around. Even the radiologists would hide!

"I've always tried to remember this and make a point of not letting myself get out of hand."

Happy Face

Dr. Mitchell

"My resident and I had been working for many hours on the technical aspects of treating several difficult cancer cases. We were contouring a patient's bowel and rectum.

"*Contouring* is when we define the areas and outline them in three dimensions. We do this to design a treatment that will give as little radiation as possible to the surrounding tissue.

"In this particular case we wanted to protect the patient's prostate and bladder, as well as spare the rectum as much as we could. We made careful diagrams to help us point the radiation beams accurately, so they wouldn't scatter and damage other areas.

"An image of the patient's abdomen was displayed on a monitor while we worked. Of course there was some gas and stool in the patient's bowels. This is perfectly normal. Gas shows up as black and the bits of stool appear as lighter grays and whites.

"After some time had passed, one of us noticed that the way the bowels and stool had been imaged made a perfect happy face. This was at the end of a long, exhausting day or it wouldn't have registered on either of us, but at the time it made for a nice moment of comic relief.

"We had twenty or thirty years of higher education between us, a Ph.D., two M.D.s, years of specialty training and fellowships, and we were both sitting there being entertained by an image of a happy face in a guy's bowel.

"It sounds silly, but sometimes it's the little things like this that keep you human. Taking a few seconds to smile, even if it's at something foolish, makes it possible for you to keep going."

***

"We use an invisible means to make things visible."

***

SKELETON CREW
Getting Experience

The practice of medicine requires a hands-on apprenticeship. Learning to stand face-to-face with difficult situations while remaining calm and positive is not easy.

Hope, Help, Heal

Dr. Paulsen

"During my residency training when I was learning to be an attending physician in radiation oncology, I treated lymphoma patients, some of whom had very bad disease.

"A lady in her late-thirties came in with a cutaneous problem, a skin problem. I looked at her file, read everything, and was ready to go examine her when the nurses stopped me. They knew I was inexperienced with these sorts of cases, and they wanted me to be careful.

"They warned me that there were tumors all over the woman's body and they explained that because of this the entire room smelled foul. None of this was the patient's fault, of course. She wasn't able to deal with these problems herself. No one could've. It simply wasn't possible.

"I went into the room forewarned and was immediately grateful that the nurses had prepared me as well as they could. It was the most horrible smell I'd ever encountered.

"My patient had lesions around her eyes, ears, and neck. It was the worst disease I could ever have imagined. I was unprepared to see that kind of disease.

"I was trying to keep my composure, to be professional, but it was shocking, and my emotions were crashing in on me. All of my training had been very scientific. I'd never faced something like this.

"I was nauseated and afraid I would throw up, but I told myself I had a moral obligation to care for this woman. I felt sorry for her and I silently prayed for her. I tried to imagine what it must be like to go through life with this condition.

"I could tell she was deeply embarrassed about her appearance. She was so ashamed she'd covered herself as fully as possible. She was wearing a coat in the middle of summer in Memphis to try to cloak the smell. Only her eyes were showing.

"I had a *what have I gotten myself into* moment, but I did what I was supposed to do. I took a history and performed an exam and I took my time.

"I did my best to put her at ease and give her reassurance. I knew the literature on her condition. I didn't make false promises, but I provided some hope. I tried to be a friend, someone who was there to help her.

"Her case was completely uncharted territory.

"I talked to senior colleagues who said things like, 'It's a waste of time' or

'Nothing will work' and 'Good luck.'

"One professor said, 'You can try. There's nothing to lose. It's up to you. Neither way is wrong.'

"I knew I could give up and do nothing, but if I did it would leave her with no further options. I was her last hope.

"I decided I would try. I wanted to give her a chance, and hope for the best, so I laid out a game plan.

"It resulted in the most satisfying experience I have ever had. Her skin responded so nicely to the radiation. It transformed her from a monster into a nice young African-American female.

"Her face, head, and neck cleared up. She came back in six weeks later and then again twelve weeks later. The last time she was wearing a tank top and her face was shining. She had the most beautiful smile.

"It was wonderful to see my patient happy and smiling and speaking to everyone. The first time I saw her all you could see was her eyes. I thought of her as *Owl Eyes* because that was what she'd looked like, hiding under her coat.

"We still talk about that lady.

"That case helped me to grow professionally. I learned how important hope is. I learned to *never* give up on a patient. And I learned a lot about myself.

"You make the effort, you do your best, and time will tell you if you made the right decision or not. Your patients are your best teachers."

"In a subsequent case, a man in his forties came in with a huge melanoma, a horrific tumor that had eroded through his face and neck. There was a foul smell coming from his oozing open sores.

"You pray that things like this don't happen to people and I silently prayed for him. I was grateful that I'd had the previous case where a woman with a different diagnosis, but an equally difficult condition, had gotten a wonderful result. That case prepared me to go forward with this one.

"'We'll do the best we can,' I said, and I was able to make a very dramatic difference for this patient. That's what made the case unique.

"In other cases I make *some* difference. I can help with the pain, for example. I'm able to reduce the person's suffering. But I might not be able to cure the disease or make it go away.

"I can help *most* people, some more than others. It's very meaningful to be able to make a dramatic improvement in a patient's life.

"I was very fortunate with my first tough case. It taught me to *never* give up."

"I treated a young patient from rural Georgia who had four children. She had brain metastasis. She'd been given three to six months to live.

"Because of the treatment I gave her she was still alive three years later. She passed away during the fourth year, but she was happy and smiling in the interim and even at the end.

"I've treated a ninety-one-year-old who wanted to live for six more months so she could see a granddaughter get married. Two years later she's still around and has seen a great granddaughter get married, as well.

"Cases like these are very satisfying. They help me find meaning in my work.

"I gave up a successful career in nuclear engineering, in health physics, to do this. With radiation I can stop bleeding. I can slow the growth-rate of a tumor. I can stop wounds from oozing. I can eliminate suffering for patients who will survive and in those who don't survive.

"For multiple myeloma patients, narcotics might not relieve all the pain, but with radiation, I have an eighty to ninety percent chance to remove the pain.

"I had a multiple myeloma patient who was in agony. It was so bad he asked me for a gun. I told him I couldn't cure his disease, but I could probably help him with the pain, and I did. Now he sends me a Christmas card every year."

"A Hispanic lady came in blind. She had multiple myeloma in her brain. I treated her and later I encountered her running down a hallway toward me, saying, 'I can see, I can see!'

"I can't cure everyone, but even in the worst cases the patient's quality of life can be greatly improved. That's why I do this."

"I had a patient who was paralyzed and unconscious, totally out of it. She had leukemia with infiltration to the brain and spinal cord.

"She was only twenty-six years old and was the mother of two young kids. Her husband sat beside her bed, crying.

"I knew that with too much radiation she would get sicker, so I went a little off-textbook and gave her three low-dose treatments. I just *tried*.

"Three days later she woke up, then afterwards she was able to walk again.

"It was so rewarding. I turned a patient who was dying, into a person who was able to leave the hospital. And now, three years later, she's still alive and doing well. She had chemotherapy and a transplant.

"I was just trying to help reduce her symptoms, not to cure her. I was just trying to give her and her husband hope. She can't remember any of it. She was too sick. But her husband cried again after she improved, this time on my shoulder."

"There was a woman in her eighties on the palliative medicine floor. She had very bad uterine cancer and it had spread. She was having frequent urinary infections and was in pain. She was suffering. Gradually she became unconscious.

"She'd been on the ward for two or three weeks, and the end was getting close. During this time there were some unpleasant family dynamics going on.

"My patient was from California. She had three daughters who lived in three different cities. There was a lot of tension among the family members. None of the daughters were ready to let their mother pass away.

"I got a sense that the mom was trying to stay for them. Her vital signs would change when her daughters were around. I could feel the tension when they were in the room.

"I decided to speak to them about it. I sat down with the daughters and talked about the family dynamics. The youngest child was the mother's favorite. The oldest was alienated from the mother. And the middle one was trying to keep them all together.

"They'd never been a cohesive group of three. There had always been discord. But it needed to stop.

"'Don't fight in this room,' I said. 'Believe it or not your mom can still feel that. She can sense it. She's a human being. Maybe she can't see herself leaving the earth until you guys are content.'

"That conversation really helped a lot. The daughters made an agreement about how to behave in their mother's room. The youngest said she would let her mom go. We all hugged and I could sense the tension disappearing.

"Their mother didn't suffer any more after that. She became calm and relaxed and then, within twenty-four hours, she passed away.

"A day or two later one of her daughters came up and hugged me again and cried on my shoulder.

"Helping families face the reality that someone is going to die is important. The person who is dying has already accepted it, but they need to know that their family has accepted it, too."

Shooting People

Young radiologists spend years mastering the exotic technologies needed to produce medical images and treat disease. They learn to use the computerized voice recognition systems and navigate the digitized image archives. At the same time they must find ways to deal diplomatically with patients as well as other doctors.

Here are some memorable moments and hard lessons—the highs and lows of the day-to-day job of a radiologist. The vignettes run the gamut from interesting to scary, and from amusing to traumatic.

Dr. Blackman

"Radiologists create images by shooting people with x-rays, sound waves, radio waves in a magnetic field, and by injecting tiny amounts of nuclear materials.

"Our pictures reveal things no one else will ever get to see. That means we have to stay sharp in case we come across something totally unexpected.

"Once I was asked to do an MRI of a man's head and I saw a tumor in the naso-pharynx on the scout film. A scout film isn't a diagnostic image. It's a film we do to position the head.

"We use it to make sure the technical aspects of study will be okay, and that the images we're planning to take will be in the correct place.

"When we saw the scout image for this patient we knew the problem wasn't up high in the guy's head where we'd been told to shoot, but down near his tonsils!

"I often find myself dictating more about what I'm seeing around the edges of a frame than what's in the center. The referring physician may be zeroing in on the wrong place, so we have to watch out for that and help guide them to the important areas."

"Radiologists need to know *everything*! The only physicians who have to know more than radiologists are the general practitioners and the pathologists.

"It's the opposite of what most people think. We need the really good guys, the *smart* guys, to go into general practice.

"Anybody can make a decent specialist. Anyone can eventually learn to get good at *one thing*."

Gosh, Look at All these Colors!

Dr. McKinney

"The most stressful situation I ever got into was when I was working on a prominent guy in my community. I was trying to visualize his vertebral artery.

"During the procedure the device that injected the contrast material malfunctioned. It injected twice as much dye as it should've.

"My patient, who was lying on the table, said, 'Gosh, look at all these colors!' Then he went totally blind.

"It took six hours for his sight to come back.

"That was a terrible feeling, a *very long* wait, wondering if my patient would ever be able to see again.

"He recovered fully, but since then I've always done the injections by hand. I could never trust a mechanical injector to function properly after that."

"The patient begins to die in radiology"

While preparing to write this book I came across a warning several times in medical commentaries: The patient begins to die in radiology. *I didn't understand what it meant, so I asked the doctors.*

Dr. Benson

"I've had patients die in the scanner.

"Usually it happens on account of a breathing or lung problem like pneumonia. When they lay down flat on the table it restricts their breathing enough that they go into respiratory failure and die.

"I've had patients react to the contrast medium, too.

"It's rare, but some people will have an anaphylactoid reaction to the dye. If that happens you have to hurry up and finish the procedure before they die.

"Their larynx will swell and close off their breathing or they'll have a vascular collapse. I've had to resuscitate people because of this. Luckily my department was adjacent to the emergency room so instant help was usually available.

"It can get frantic. When you've got someone in anaphylactic shock it's certainly a time of heightened activity. People are going in all directions. You have to have good team coordination.

"Everyone needs to know what to do and when to do it. You have to know when to give the patient some adrenalin, and when to get them intubated. It's good to practice the sequence every once in a while.

"I've seen too many times where they'll bring a crash cart but forget to bring the key to the drug box. The medicines in the cart are kept locked up, which means you can find yourselves locked out of critical supplies at the worst possible time.

"I don't want that to ever happen to me again. For that reason I always keep a fresh syringe of adrenalin taped to my CT machine."

Level 1 Trauma

Dr. Kerr

"We see *severe* trauma at LeBonheur.

"We're the only Pediatric Level 1 Trauma Center for over 200 miles. That means some of our patients get flown in.

"Some of them aren't hurt too bad and they bounce back. Other times, despite rapid, aggressive, maximal care, the children don't survive. Or if they do survive, they have major deficits.

"The initial survey gets done before the child comes to us, but they will often still be in the midst of resuscitation efforts when they arrive in radiology.

"If they can't be out of someone's direct hands, they don't come to us. They have to be temporarily stabilized, able to survive for at least a minute or two while not having medical personnel actively working on them, so they can be in the scanner.

"If you aren't careful and don't keep close eyes on these kids, you can have problems with the ones who are unstable, or sick, or who have something unclear going on. Patients have to be closely monitored when they are with us in radiology.

"Sometimes these children are in our care when something unexpected happens, but that's rare."

"Level 1 trauma centers will sometimes need to scan people who are very seriously injured, who've been in a bad car wreck, and come in on a helicopter. These people might be considered DOAs in another hospital, or they might get immediate exploratory surgery, but that can be really dangerous.

"Fifteen years ago the standard of care for a trauma patient who had any signs of an abdominal injury, or who needed to have blood taken out of their abdomen, was to do exploratory surgery. That meant they opened the abdomen and took a look around.

"They might go in and see that everything's fine. Or they might open the patient and have a great gush of blood and see that the spleen has been shattered. Patients can die from this kind of exploratory surgery.

"But now the surgeons can get an idea of what they will need to deal with before they start the surgery.

"Over time we've learned other things with our scans that help avoid surgery—like that you don't have to operate on mild injuries to the spleen. You can follow the patient's blood count for a few hours instead.

"That insight has saved lives."

Get in and Get Out

Dr. Hoffman

"Interventional radiology has procedures that are complicated and tedious—like when you're running catheters down blood vessels, looking for an AVM, an arteriovenous malformation.

"You have to be careful what you're putting into a blood vessel, particularly in the brain. You have to be fast and smooth. The longer you stay in there the more apt the patient is to throw a clot, so you have to work efficiently.

"Before you start, you make sure you have everything you might need readily available, so you won't have to stop and look for something during the procedure.

"You learn these things over the years. You get better with experience.

"You get gray hair from some of the harder lessons."

Don't Pet the Cat

Dr. Weiss

"CTs used to be called *CAT scans*.

"But then PET scanners were invented and we began to use the two technologies together. We use the CAT scans to create anatomical maps that we overlay on the PET image to help us interpret the picture.

"The hybrid image might've been called CAT-PET or PET-CAT but that didn't sound very impressive. It certainly didn't sound like an expensive cutting-edge technology.

"So we had to stop saying CAT and start saying CT to prevent people from saying *PET the CAT*."

Risk

Dr. Manning

"There's a risk in doing things to a patient and there's a risk in *not* doing things.

"We are always asking ourselves, *What's the safest way to get the information we need to treat this patient?*

"There's a study you can do to look for pulmonary embolism. But these patients might be on blood thinners and that makes them vulnerable to surgical procedures. Any interventions on these patients become more dangerous on account of the possibility of bleeding.

"Now we can do a CT first, to see if the person really needs the study or not. It's safer for the patient that way. But even then, there's a chance of mortality in these people while they're in the radiology department getting the CT.

"It's in the nature of pulmonary embolism cases that these patients are the sickest people. They will sometimes *code*, their heart or their breathing will stop on the way to the radiology department or while they're inside the department.

"But the reality is that these patients would have coded, died, even if they hadn't come to us, because coding is the natural trajectory of their disease process. It might be more accurate to say, 'The patient *finishes* dying in the radiology department.'

"At this hospital we don't deal with a lot of patients who are normal and healthy. We aren't doing a chest x-ray on someone with a cough, or a scan on someone with a headache. Here, we're dealing mostly with cancer.

"The issue we're facing most often is: has the tumor grown or has it responded to treatment.

"So, do we have patients die in radiology? Yes, we do."

Dyeing Man

Dr. Lowe

"A man in his mid-thirties came in with abdominal pain and edema in his intestines. I asked for a CT scan and he agreed to that, but he refused to let us administer the contrast dye that would delineate the vascular structures.

"It's rare, but some people are allergic to the contrast medium, and if they are, that can cause serious problems. This patient had no history to indicate he'd have any problems with it, and I believed we needed the dye to get a diagnosis.

"It took a while, but I was eventually able to talk him into having the contrast injection. When we injected the dye it illuminated the vascular structures and I was able to see the problem. It was a thrombosed superior mesenteric vein.

"If we hadn't used the contrast medium, he would've died—unless he'd had exploratory surgery and they'd been able to find the problem—but he might have died from the exploratory surgery."

***

"We can find more problems now.
But we can't fix everything we can find."

***

Don't Scan Yourself

Dr. Duval

"Radiologists have to know not only disease processes, but also anatomy, and, most importantly, they have to know what *normal* looks like.

"*Normal* isn't a narrow, clearly- defined set of presentations you can memorize. Normal encompasses a high degree of variation.

"A lot of abnormalities aren't significant, but non-significant abnormalities can appear very different, so it's not always easy to recognize them.

"There's also a lot of variation in the way significant abnormalities look. It's not always easy to tell the difference here either. But the key to being a good radiologist is being able to recognize which is which.

"A lot of people live well with abnormalities. There are developmental abnormalities that make no difference in the patient's health, like organ reversals or unusual positions that don't affect the patient's wellbeing."

"I often need normal images to teach the residents with, like an MRI of a normal cervical spine. So during my free time I used to scan myself to generate these images. Then one day I found a thyroid nodule on myself.

"Now I tell people, *Just don't look.*

"At some point we all think, *Don't go to the hospital. If you do they'll find something wrong with you.*

"When you do a CT of the abdomen, sometimes you'll pick up a tumor in the kidney or pancreas, or an aortic aneurysm.

"Five percent of people who die have an aneurysm, but most of those people didn't die because of the aneurysm.

"You ask yourself, *Is this one going to cause a problem?* The answer is, *Probably not.*

"Brain surgery is required to fix things in the brain.

"Unfortunately any intervention they do in your brain can change you just a little bit. If something happens to me and I'm conscious enough to speak, I'll say, 'Don't do it.'

"Sure, you want to treat hydrocephalus or certain emergencies with brain surgery, but you don't want to do brain surgery on *all* of them. It's a big deal to find out what that *thing* is when it's in your brain."

Bad Decision-Making

Dr. Hayes

"When you're trying to make a decision about whether to have surgery or not, if you're in pain your decision-making will get skewed by the pain.

"Your body has a natural tendency to fuse a degenerative disc. This means that *on its own* your body will do the same thing that a surgeon would do, but the surgeons do it faster.

"Patients tend to hear what they want to hear. They'll get surgery if there's even a *chance* it will help. No matter how small that chance is.

"All day I see the bad back surgeries, the failed backs. In cases where there's a bulging disc I know if these people would just wait, maybe their pain would go away on its own, without surgery.

"If you have back pain and no trauma, don't look! Don't take an image for six weeks or longer, because you'll always see *something*. Everybody has degenerative disc disease.

"You can make a choice to ignore the pain in the short term. Pain is a bad decision-making environment."

"When you're looking at radiological images of backs it can be especially difficult to correlate what the radiologist is seeing with the situation as the patient is describing it.

"I'll see things that look like they need to be fixed, but the patient will say they're fine—they're having no pain and no problems with the activities of daily life. Some people have a back that looks like a wreck to us, but they're out in the world working every day with no complaint.

"I've also seen things that are hardly worth noticing, but the patient's unable to function. Some people with the smallest visible problems will be in terrible pain or even confined to bed.

"The variation of *normal* is enormous."

Rocket Man

Dr. Young

"When I worked in central Florida, we could watch NASA launch rockets from the top two floors of the hospital.

"The people who pilot rockets and spaceships are an utterly unique category of patients. Their medical conditions were the most highly polarized I've ever seen.

"There didn't seem to be any middle ground for these people. They were either *fine* or *dead*."

High-Impact Sports

Radiologists sometimes end up as patients in their own departments. Some of them have more of a tendency to do this than others. One of the radiologists I spoke to loved to drive fast, race motorcycles, and fly high-performance hang gliders. And over the years he had a lot of high-speed encounters with the ground.

Dr. Andrews

"I've had four or five wrecks, but only one serious one.

"In the bad one I broke nine ribs, a scapula, crushed my lungs, dinged my spleen, and got a head injury.

"I've had two hang glider crashes. Both times I ended up at Erlanger—one because I got knocked out, and the other because I broke an arm.

"I have two screws in my left leg. I have a total hip replacement on the right side. I have two plates and a bolt in my arm.

"I wrecked a Segway.

"I've had three car wrecks that I can remember."

Different Strokes

Dr. Harper

"When a person has the oxygen to their brain cut off, that's essentially a stroke. But not all strokes are equal. They can happen in different ways and each type produces a different pattern of damage.

"A stroke can be caused by a blood clot in a vessel, or atherosclerosis, or plaques. These types of strokes are often confined to a specific area. They impair the blood supply from the particular artery that's clotted off.

"If the patient has low blood pressure, the parts of the brain near the big arteries will get oxygen, but the areas farther way won't get as much.

"When a person drowns nearly all of the brain gets injured. But the cerebellum, the hindbrain, tends to use a little less oxygen than the forebrain, so the cerebellum might get spared, relatively.

"You can tell from looking at an image of the brain whether the person was drowned or had a blood clot. The pictures look different."

"I love neuroradiology. I particularly enjoy visualizing vessels. I love to be able to contribute understanding as to why a patient feels the way they do. I love knowing that I'm helping someone, making a positive difference in someone's life.

"A lot of the vascular stuff can be fixed with medicine.

"I love to see something and realize, *Oh, I know what's going on!*

"One example of this is when a patient who has had a stomach bypass isn't able to absorb all their vitamins properly because they have a shorter gut. They can get serious problems from it like Wernicke's encephalopathy and Korsakoff's syndrome.

"They can get memory loss and an inability to make new memories, but these problems can be treated with intravenous vitamins if the situation is caught early enough.

"The ability to diagnose things like that makes my job satisfying."

Porcelain

Dr. Todd

"I've had a lot of satisfying cases over the years.

"One was a lady who came in with blood clot in an artery in her leg. She had what's called *porcelain leg*. They call it that because when the circulation is cut off the limb becomes totally white.

"When you see something like that you know the blood flow has probably been stopped for so long the muscles are irreversibly damaged. If you're able to reestablish blood flow to the limb, the toxins from the necrotic tissue can cause kidney failure.

"This patient needed to be infused with a clot buster or she was going to lose her leg, and maybe even her life. So I snaked a catheter down and put it right into the clot. This was a special type of catheter with small holes in the sides. I pushed the clot buster medicine out through those holes so it would infuse the clot.

"I sat up with her and sprayed the clot *all night long*.

"It worked.

"Her leg swelled up, and she had to go into the ICU for a while, but she lived, and her leg was saved.

"After that she sent me a Christmas card every year for fifteen years.

"Any time you save somebody's leg with an angiographic procedure, when you see them after you've found something that's fixable like the narrowing of an artery before a possible stroke, and you've repaired it, you get a great deal of satisfaction.

"I've been able to do that twenty to thirty times."

No Patience With Patients

Dr. Jayashankar

"A friend of mine in the pulmonary program told me that the Fellows met one morning and one of them asked, 'Do we really have to go see the patient today?'

"He wanted to treat his patient by looking at a computer and studying his data.

"Radiologists encounter this kind of thing a lot—doctors who want to diagnose and treat a patient without actually having to see them or examine them. They hope we can tell them everything without their having to ever meet the patient."

Radiological Humor

"How do you hide $5 from a radiologist?

"You put it on a patient."

Herding Cats

Dr. Bennett

"Radiologists work for other physicians.

"We are physicians' physicians.

"This means we have to be able to handle doctors, which is like herding cats.

"Some doctors like for you to examine the patient and even do certain procedures, like a biopsy. Others don't want you touching the patient or even talking to them.

"Radiologists who work in a hospital have a captive audience. Radiologists who are in private practice have to get along with the other doctors.

"We do a lot of consulting. Patients think their doctor diagnosed them, but really the radiologist made the diagnosis. Patients rarely see the contribution a radiologist makes.

"We work in the background where nobody notices us, but we save a lot of lives. We catch things. We solve problems.

"We render a tremendous service to the patient and the physician.

"Most of the time the patients never think about the radiologist. We're laboring in a world of our own, back there in a room somewhere.

"We don't work for recognition. It's a service specialty."

"That feeling of going into a reading room is magical. I never get tired of it.

"Every day I get to see *through* people, see *inside* them.

"We're an amazing machine. I love getting to look at us everyday and see how we're made and how the body works.

"What I'm looking at isn't just an image, though. It's not like abstract art. You don't look at a radiograph and say, 'I just saw my brain, and I loved it.'

"I've seen two radiologists totally disagree about the interpretation of an image, about whether it's a disease process or not. There are benign things that look horrible, and malignancies that look benign until it's too late.

"We have to treat the patient and not the pictures.

"To interpret an image you might need to observe how things are changing over time. You might need to compare one picture to another to understand what you're seeing.

"Scary things change.

"You have to monitor yourself when you're at work and be aware that what you see when you look at an image can depend on how you're feeling, for instance if you just read a normal case or if you just read a horrible one.

"And there are certain other things you learn to watch out for, too. For example, I always look at the patient's age and look for signs that they've led a hard life.

"If they're thirty and have bad lungs, I know they smoke, and I know that means they will have a totally different medical situation."

The Business of Medicine

Dr. Loveday

"Medicine went from being a humanitarian profession run by individual doctors to a cash flow business run by huge corporations and the government. It makes no sense, but doctors have been gradually removed from the system.

"The practice of medicine is now controlled by hospitals, insurance companies, and the government. That has caused an enormous increase in the cost of care.

"Now patients have to pay the salaries of all these non-medical middlemen. Increasing premiums aren't funding medical care, they're funding this new burgeoning administrative bureaucracy.

"The coding system and computerized billing have caused medicine to become focused on having expensive technical procedures done, rather than spending time talking with your physician. Hospitals make more money that way.

"When you remove both the buyer and the seller from the equation you get gross price distortions. That's what we have now. Doctors are just beasts of burden in today's system. Patients are just chess pieces to be moved through an automated system.

"Physicians have been forced into such rigid structures that a young doctor now finds it impossible to open his own practice. He *has* to join a preexisting group.

"There used to be fewer barriers to access to medical care, the doctor might not get paid, but everyone could see the doctor. The poor weren't denied care.

"The new mechanized, institutionally-run system has changed this."

"The appealing part of medicine for me was the independence.

"When I started out you could make your own decisions. But that's not true anymore. Now hospitals pressure doctors to order lots of tests.

"Tests are easier to deal with using computerized accounting and they have a higher profit margin. Now only sixteen cents of every medical dollar spent goes to doctors.

"Because of this I retired early and went back to teach part-time. I still love medicine, but I refuse to practice in the current system."

***

Skeleton:
A bunch of bones with the person scraped off.

***

FUNNY BONE
X-Ray Bloopers

Although the practice of medicine is usually a sober endeavor, ridiculous circumstances arise with refreshing regularity. Here are a few comical vignettes that demonstrate the distinctive brand of bloopers that can arise only in radiology.

Insert Coins Here

Dr. Wesley

"An older lady came in with gastrointestinal symptoms.

"We did an upper and lower GI series. We looked at her small bowel and did a barium enema.

"I examined the images and could see that she had swallowed some coins. They were clearly visible inside her.

"When I gave her the diagnosis, she got irate. She accused me of putting the coins in there.

"She said, 'I know you did it because you asked me if I had any change in my bowel habits before you even took those pictures!'

"I was never able to convince her that I hadn't put the coins inside her."

Loose Change

Dr. Park

"It's not uncommon for us to see images of a young child or a mentally imbalanced adult who has ingested a coin.

"The craziest radiological image I ever saw was of a guy who had a compulsion to swallow any and every coin he came across. He had an enormous number of them in his stomach.

"It eventually got to the point where his stomach couldn't empty properly, so he had to be operated on and have the coins removed.

"The post-surgery x-ray generated my favorite radiological report of all time. It said, 'Impression: *No change.*'"

Radiological Arts and Crafts

Dr. Jackson

"A lady came in to have some x-rays taken. She'd already made her own diagnosis, but she wanted us to confirm it.

"'I have Rupert worms,' she said.

"If you look up *Rupert worms* you can find an entry for an historical person, St. Rupert of Worms, Bishop of Salzburg, but there aren't any medical conditions with that name.

"We x-rayed the lady and read the images. We didn't see anything wrong with her. When she received our findings she came back to the office and requested copies of her films.

"We gave them to her and she left.

"She took the x-rays home and decorated one of them. She drew on it with a red marker and cut up pieces of fabric and glued them onto the film to show us the Rupert worms we'd missed.

"She'd obviously spent a lot of time on her project. Then she brought the film back in and gave it to me. She'd confirmed her own diagnosis and she wanted me to see it.

"It was an amazing picture. I kept it in my office for many years."

Needle in a Haystack

Dr. Turner

When I was a senior radiology resident at Jackson Memorial Hospital in Miami our Department Chairman got a phone call from a trainer at Hialeah Race Track.

One of his racehorses had an inflamed leg and he had taped a radium source to the animal's leg to treat the problem. This was a typical treatment in those days.

Unfortunately the source had fallen off the horse's leg, and he couldn't find it. My boss told me to get a Geiger counter and drive out to Hialeah and search for it.

The radium source was about two or three inches long and had the diameter of a small pencil. Radium has a half-life of 1,620 years. If the horse had stepped on the source and broken it, there could be very dangerous radiation contamination to the area.

The clean up would be a nightmare. It might require extensive and widespread measures.

The trainer had been wise enough to remove the horse from its stall, but the floor was full of dirty hay, horse poop, and the like.

It took me about ten minutes of poking around in the manure, but I found the radium source and it was intact.

Radium is no longer used for these kinds of problems, but in the early to mid-1900s there were all sorts of quack cures that relied on radiation to treat everything from hemorrhoids, to deafness, to cataracts.

There were radioactive cigarette holders that were supposed to improve your complexion while you smoked, and radioactive toothpaste that was sold to treat gingivitis and for tooth whitening.

We've gotten a lot smarter since then.

Wrong Place, Wrong Tine

Dr. Henry

"A guy was driving down I-4 behind a landscaper's truck when a pitchfork fell off and landed on the pavement in front of him.

"There was no way for him to avoid the thing, so he had to try to drive over it. Unfortunately his car didn't have much ground clearance. The pitchfork got jammed underneath his vehicle and the tines harpooned up through the floorboard on the driver's side.

"The prongs speared through the accelerator pedal and the bottom of the guy's shoe, stabbing him, and continued through his foot. The metal tips of two tines were sticking out the top of his shoe.

"He was impaled on the accelerator, zooming along a busy stretch of interstate at sixty miles an hour, trapped by a nightmarish version of cruise control.

"The guy had the presence of mind to turn the ignition off, so the car slowed down, then he managed to steer it out of the driving lanes and onto the shoulder of the interstate.

"He couldn't get out of the car, though, because his foot was stapled to the accelerator. This was back in the days before cell phones, so the best he could do was roll his window down and wave like a maniac until someone finally stopped to help him.

"An emergency crew arrived and men crawled underneath the car. They sawed the wooden handle off the pitchfork, removed pieces of the floorboard, and dismantled the accelerator mechanism. They were eventually able to separate the guy from his car.

"They put him on a stretcher with the long metal spikes still sticking through his shoe and part of the accelerator. They draped a sheet across him from the waist down and took him to the hospital.

"Before attempting to pull the pitchfork loose, the emergency room doctor sent the patient to radiology to get more information about the internal damage to his foot. When he arrived at the radiology department the x-ray technician flipped the sheet back and told the guy, 'You gotta take your shoe off.'

"A few moments of chaos and panic followed that suggestion, during which the patient strenuously objected to anyone pulling on anything, so the tech agreed to take the x-ray with everything intact.

"The film showed that there were two pieces of metal stabbed through the guy's foot, which wasn't news. But it also revealed that despite the significant soft tissue injuries, miraculously, no bones had been damaged.

"The patient had to be taken to surgery and put to sleep so they could pull the pitchfork out and remove his shoe.

"After that he did fine."

Training Films

Dr. Clay

"Radiologists see a *lot* of foreign objects inside people. They might be anywhere in the body. Some of them enter through the skin and others arrive through the various bodily orifices. Most of these cases come to us via the emergency room.

"One of the cases I use as a teaching tool concerns a fellow who came to the ER one evening when I was in training. I show my residents the x-ray we took. The image shows a guy with a plastic banana in his colon.

"The doctor on duty that night told the man, 'I can probably get it out with forceps,' but the guy didn't like the sound of that, so he left the hospital in a huff.

"An hour later he came back.

"I show my residents the x-ray we took of the guy on his second trip to the ER. Now he had a banana and a screwdriver in his colon.

"This time he agreed to let the ER doctor help him."

"A couple of years later another guy came into the ER with a screwdriver up his rectum. No plastic banana this time, just a screwdriver. I had experience now and it was up to me to handle the situation.

"I told the patient I'd remove the screwdriver for him, and I did.

"I was about to toss it into a waste container when the patient told me he wanted the screwdriver back. He said he needed it for his work.

"I'd never been asked to return a foreign body removed from an orifice before, but I understood the guy's dilemma, so I washed it off and gave it back to him.

"He thanked me and went on his way."

"I've seen more than one person who attempted to reduce their hemorrhoids with a Coke bottle.

"They'd squat down over the bottle, hoping to push the hemorrhoids back up inside their rectum, but at some point during the procedure they lost their balance.

"It's possible for an entire Coke bottle to go into the colon.

"Once the big end of the bottle gets past the sphincter muscles, it's not something you can deal with by yourself."

Dressing

Dr. Berenson

"I was an x-ray technician for several years. It was a lot easier to blend in as female tech than it was later when I became a radiologist. I'm not sure why but radiology is one of the specialties that's still very heavily populated by men.

"It's a normal part of the job for an x-ray tech to ask patients to change clothes. I took a gentleman to the changing area, put him behind the curtain, handed him a gown, and told him to remove his clothes and put on the gown.

"I came back a few minutes later, stuck my head into the room, and told the man to come out from behind the curtain and follow me. I walked ahead of him down the hall, opened the door to the x-ray room, and then turned around, holding the door open, expecting him to follow me inside.

"But when I looked back, I saw that the guy was totally naked. He'd apparently misunderstood my instructions to *put on the gown*. I could feel myself turning red.

"I tried to speak, but I couldn't, so I just grabbed the man by the wrist, pulled him inside the x-ray room, and shut the door on him. Then I ran to get him a gown.

"I handed it inside the x-ray room and asked him to put it on. When he'd had time to get the gown on I went back into the room to take his x-rays.

"By this point he'd realized he'd made an embarrassing mistake and he was even redder than me.

"I took the pictures and then made myself scarce. I didn't want to be anywhere in sight when he left. It would've been too embarrassing for either of us to see each other again."

"You wouldn't think the gowning process was that difficult, but apparently it is because that wasn't the only time I had a problem with a male patient.

"I went through the same set of instructions with another guy, only this one was much younger. He was in his early twenties.

"After that first incident I always made sure to tell people *plainly* to put the gown on. This particular examination gown was one of the newer styles. It had three armholes.

"I admit they can be hard to figure out, especially the first time you're trying to get one on. But they're made that way so they'll wrap all the way around the patient and close without needing any ties or snaps. This style will protect a person's modesty better than the other ones—if you get it on right.

"I waited for the patient to change and then went in to get him. He stuck his head out from behind the curtain and motioned for me to come over.

"I don't know how he did it, but somehow he'd gotten his *head* through one of the armholes! Then he'd tried to get his arms through the other two holes. He's gotten stuck in an awkward configuration with most of the gown behind his back.

"There was no way for him pull the flaps of the gown together enough to cover his private parts without choking himself. But he couldn't get free either because both arms were pinned behind his back.

"He needed my help, immediately.

"I ran to get some scissors and as quickly as possible I cut the gown off him, starting at his neck so he could breathe. Then I brought him another gown and helped him put it on the right way.

"This time I didn't get overly embarrassed or feel like I needed to sneak away after I took the x-rays. I'd learned to sympathize with the patient.

"Going to the doctor and being given a lot of unfamiliar instructions puts people in a vulnerable position. I understood that and wanted to be as helpful as I could.

"You gradually learn to act more professional and handle things with a good poker face. That works better for everyone."

Kidnapping

Dr. Elliott

"I was called out of bed and asked to come to the hospital in the middle of the night to reduce an intussusception. That's a life-threatening bowel problem in a baby where one part of their intestine slides inside another part, like the sections of a telescope being collapsed into each other.

"When this situation arises, it needs to be fixed right away.

"I got to the x-ray department and waited for the little boy to be brought down from the third floor. That was the way things were handled at the time.

"I waited and waited, but the baby didn't show up. This was in the wee hours of the morning, and there weren't a lot of people around, so I decided I'd go get the patient myself.

"I went upstairs and picked up the baby. There was a woman on duty when I got him and I thought she understood what was happening, but apparently she didn't.

"As I carried the little guy down to the radiology department I heard on the hospital loudspeaker, 'Paging Dr. Steel, Dr. Steel.'

"This was the warning that was broadcasted when someone was attempting to steal a baby. There were several different versions of these coded alerts. If there was a fire they'd page *Doctor Red*. If there was a bad guy roaming around they'd page *Dr. Roam* and give a description.

"The phone rang just as I got to radiology and I answered it, suspecting what the call was about. A pediatric nurse said, 'We can't send the baby down because some strange man came in and kidnapped him!'

"I explained that it wasn't a strange man, it was me. I told her I had the baby and there had *not* been a kidnapping.

"I did the study and the corrective procedure and was able to fix the little boy's problem so he would be able to eat and digest his food properly. It was a frustrating and exhausting night, but the little boy did fine.

"Some cases are easier than others."

Barium

Dr. Sinclair

"We were doing a study that required a barium enema.

"When we do these we have a bag of contrast medium, liquid barium, hanging on a pole next to the patient. We use it to fill up the colon, then we examine the person with a fluoroscope so we can see what's happening.

"When we're doing the procedure I'll say to the technician, 'Barium on,' to let the tech know that I'm unclamping the tube that will allow the barium flow down into the patient.

"Then, when the colon is full, I'll clamp the tube to stop any more barium from draining out of the bag, and say, 'Barium off.'

"Our patient wasn't familiar with our procedures or our terminology. Unbeknownst to me, what I was saying was scaring him.

"The second time I said *barium*, he threw up his hands and hollered, 'Wait a minute, Doc! I'm not dead yet!'

"He thought I was saying, *bury him*."

Wastebasket

Dr. Garrett

"We had a female patient who needed a colon study. That meant she had to have a barium enema.

"If you load *anyone* up with a barium enema, there are predictable consequences. Sometimes there are unpredictable consequences as well. In this particular case we had both.

"When it came time for this lady to evacuate her bowels, she got confused about where she was supposed to go and made a wrong turn and missed the restroom.

"This created a *serious* problem. She needed to relieve herself pronto, but she'd accidentally gotten on the wrong corridor and this severely limited her options.

"The result was that one of our radiologists went into his office and found the lady sitting on his wastebasket evacuating her enema."

Hang Ups

Dr. Oakley

"One of our radiologists was dictating his findings on an echocardiogram. At the end of his report he thought he'd terminated the audio connection, but he hadn't.

"Without realizing he was still being recorded, he proceeded to tell a colleague about a torrid affair he was having with someone who worked at the hospital.

"He had no idea what he'd done or he could've deleted it immediately.

"Unfortunately for him the audio was retained on a central system that all the doctors and nurses could call in to and listen.

"There's no telling how many times that audio was played, but it's a safe bet that it was the most popular medical report in the history of the hospital."

Zucchini Surgery

Dr. Norton

"When you're first learning how to do an ultrasound-guided breast biopsy one of the ways you can get training is to go to a workshop.

"I went to a typical one. An eggplant was used to represent the patient. They put the eggplant on the table and made a slit in it. Then they insert an olive through the slit to simulate a different type of tissue.

"An olive has a different acoustical impedance from an eggplant, so we could use the combo to practice with. By the time you got through the workshop you'd learned how to perform the ultrasound-guided procedure.

"A friend of mine who was an interventional radiologist had a lady come to him. She needed a breast biopsy. She was a doctor herself and she was also married to a doctor.

"My friend was a fearless surgeon who did a lot of cardiac work. He was very well-regarded and had great hand-eye coordination. But before this lady would let my friend touch her, she wanted to check out his credentials.

"'How many breast biopsies have you done?' she asked.

"He was a little taken aback to be queried about his competence, and replied, 'Fruits or vegetables?'

"'What?' she asked.

"'I've done one zucchini and no fruit,' he said.

"She was not impressed with his joking around, so she left without letting him perform the biopsy.

"He was telling me about the encounter, and I said, 'Why did you say that? You can't biopsy a zucchini! Nobody biopsies zucchinis. And it isn't a vegetable, it's a fruit!

"You biopsied an eggplant and an olive. They're all fruits. Your previous experience was performing biopsies on *two fruits.*'

"Then I realized what I was saying, and told him, 'You shoulda just lied.'"

Fire!

Dr. Wexler

"We were doing research, looking for ways to diagnose cancers of the vocal cords.

"One of the methods we tried involved taking a powdered form of the heavy metal tantalum and putting it in an atomizer.

"You'd grab the patient's tongue and have them breathe in xylocaine mist to numb the area. Then we'd spray the tantalum dust into their throat and take them to the fluoroscope.

"We'd have them say *eeee* and *ahhh* and take a look at what happened. The pictures we got of the larynx and vocal cords were just gorgeous, but they took *forever* to make. The time it took wasn't the only problem, either.

"Tantalum is pyrophoric. That means fire-bearing, which means it's highly explosive and will spontaneously combust in certain conditions.

"During our experiments I discovered that when a hundred percent oxygen hits tantalum powder the mixture will ignite like a blowtorch.

"This actually happened when I was performing a test on a patient. When it did, it really startled me, not to mention what it did to the patient.

"I dropped the atomizer. Then we both watched, stunned, as the thing went snaking around on the floor—on fire!

"I hollered for someone to shut it off and we were able to get it stopped before we burned the hospital down. Thank goodness the patient wasn't injured at all.

"I was fine, too, but we still decided to discontinue that particular line of research."

Wired

Dr. Nelson

"Kidneys drain through the ureter to the bladder. The ureter can get obstructed with a stone or a tumor and the backpressure from the obstruction can destroy the kidney.

"When this happens you need to put a catheter in and drain the kidney externally until the obstruction can be removed. To do this in the old days you'd roll the patient onto their belly and try to visualize the kidney on the fluoroscope. You could *sorta* see with the fluoro, but not very well.

"In one case, after a urologist put a catheter in, I sharpened the stiff end of a guide wire and fed it in through the catheter. I'm looking at the guy's back using the fluoro and I can see the kidney. The other doctor is feeding the guide wire in and he keeps pushing and pushing.

"'Do you see it yet?' he asks.

"'No,' I say, so he keeps pushing.

"I'm watching the fluoro, waiting for the wire to show up, but I still don't see anything.

"'I'm outta guide wire!' he says, finally.

"I'm thinking to myself, *That can't be. The wire's three feet long!* Then I look at the patient and notice the shoulder of his gown is moving.

"I look closer and I see that the wire has come out above the patient's scapula, his shoulder blade. That's nowhere near his kidney.

"We pulled the wire out and re-routed it. We got it right on the second try and the patient did fine."

***

"Hydrocephalus is an abnormal accumulation of cerebrospinal fluid in the brain. One way to treat it was to run a tube, a shunt, from the brain down into the abdomen. This helps drain the interconnected cavities in the brain where cerebrospinal fluid is produced, the ventricles.

"To put the shunt in, you drill a burr hole in the side of the patient's head. When you get the tube installed you take an x-ray to make sure everything is positioned correctly.

"It's a simple procedure. Usually nothing goes wrong. But in this case when we took an x-ray of the head, neck, and abdomen, we saw that instead of going down into the abdomen the tube had curved around and come back up into the patient's mouth!

"The doctors had put in an extra long catheter to allow for the youngster to grow. Somehow it had gone off course. It perforated the stomach and traveled up the esophagus, into the throat.

"The tube had a soft tip. It shouldn't have been possible for it to penetrate the stomach, but it did.

"You see things like this and you know that you couldn't have done it if you'd tried. If your life depended on it, you couldn't have done it. But it happened.

"They backed it out and repositioned it so it would work properly."

"Something similar happened with an adult. After a shunt was installed the patient said he was having trouble swallowing. We looked with the CT and saw the tubing had somehow ended up in the back of the guy's throat.

"I called the neurosurgeon to tell her what I was seeing.

"She thought I was hallucinating. She said, 'This isn't possible!'

"But it was.

"So they fixed it. A general surgeon had to come help them fix it."

Exhausted

Dr. Evans

"We were looking at x-rays and CTs of a patient who was in the ER. He'd been in a motorcycle wreck.

"The guy was blown up like a balloon. He had air distributed throughout the muscles, skin, and deeper interstitial soft tissues of his chest, abdomen, pelvis, and limbs. Even his scrotum was inflated.

"When you see something like this, if you're a radiologist, you go looking for a leak from somewhere inside the body, especially from the airways or the esophagus. We knew this guy was severely injured so we looked carefully at the images of his lungs, trachea, throat, and sinuses, but all these areas appeared to be intact.

"We were stumped. We couldn't figure out where the air was coming from. We went out to the ER to get some more information and learned that the collision had impaled the man on the exhaust pipe of the car that had been in front of him.

"That explained it.

"The excess air wasn't leaking into his tissues from *inside*, it had been pumped into him from the *outside*. He'd been inflated like a football before the EMTs could get him loose.

"The man was in the ICU for a few days until the puffiness subsided and he gradually reverted to his normal size."

Lights Out

Dr. Fletcher

"Two fertility doctors came to my office to observe a radiological study on one of their patients. They'd asked me to perform a hysterosalpingogram. That's a diagnostic exam of the uterus, fallopian tubes, and nearby areas.

"It's a special type of fluoroscopy you do on a woman who's having trouble getting pregnant. You're checking to see if the uterine cavity looks normal and if both fallopian tubes are open.

"To do the test, you put a little tube into the uterus and inject contrast medium. Some OB/GYNs just send the patient, but these doctors wanted to assess the situation first-hand.

"By this point in my career I'd done hundreds of these procedures. Some of them are easy, some are difficult. The trouble is, you never know in advance which is gonna be which.

"I put my gloves on, the patient was put in the stirrups, and I readied my tray—arranging the contrast medium, the syringe, and a balloon catheter. I put sterile gel on the speculum, inserted it, and opened it. I got my balloon catheter. Then I needed to identify the opening of the cervix, called the *os* or the *ostium,* so I could feed the tubing into the uterus.

"This was in the afternoon and a thunderstorm erupted. These storms are typical daily occurrences in Florida during certain seasons and they're usually brief, so we ignore them. Unfortunately this time a bolt of lightning struck the transformer on my office building.

"There was a huge boom, a crash, and a power failure.

"The lights went out and all the machines went off. My tech screamed and ran out of the room for reasons that weren't clear to me. And my patient screamed and snapped her legs together like a vise.

"I hadn't taken quick enough evasive action, so the woman's thighs clamped against the sides of my head with tremendous force. In an instant I became unable to see, or hear, or breathe. And she wouldn't let go!

"The fertility specialists realized what had happened and even in the total darkness they managed to forcibly extract me from between the woman's legs. But by the time they got me out, my glasses had fallen off, my hair and my shirt were all askew, and I was totally disoriented.

"I thought I'd had a stroke! I'd seen a big flash of light and then suddenly gone totally deaf and blind.

"I got myself and my patient sorted out and then, when the lights came back on, we finished the procedure. The fertility specialists told me they encountered these kinds of female reflexes frequently, so they knew how to anticipate them and take appropriate precautions.

"Radiologists—not so much.

"The doctors who there with me that day warned me after they got me out. 'Don't *ever* get in that close again,' they said. 'If you can't see the knees, *back up.*'

"After that day I never did a hysterosalpingogram without having two techs with me—one standing on either side of the patient, holding the thighs. Just in case."

The Breath of Death

When I started this book I was aware that radiology involved some extremely worrisome substances, like radioactive materials, and that it relied on dangerous devices like x-ray machines. But the more time I spent hanging out with radiologists, the more aware I became of my naiveté in regard to some of the lesser known radiological threats to public health and safety.

For example, I'd never realized that the film radiologists used until 1953 would spontaneously combust! I'd come across vague warnings about how the film stock could deteriorate over time, how it might acquire a strong stink of vinegar, and under certain conditions *could produce toxic gases so rapidly that dangerous pressures might occur inside structures.*

But reading those words in a boring textbook don't bring home the reality as well as, say, a bit of history from the Cleveland Clinic radiology department. I learned that in 1929 tens of thousands of x-rays stored in the basement of the clinic spontaneously burst into flame and then exploded, creating the effect of multiple bomb blasts.

One hundred and twenty six people were killed very quickly by poison gas from the burning films, later dubbed *The Breath of Death*, and the roof was blown off the four-story clinic building—by old x-rays.

It turns out the guy who discovered the chemistry behind what became x-ray film stock was working in his kitchen in Switzerland one day when he knocked over a bottle of nitric acid. He wiped up the spill with a cotton apron and hung the apron near a stove to dry. Some unspecified interval later there was a flash and the apron exploded.

This tendency to explode without warning was no deterrent to the explosives industry. They were thrilled and used the new information to great effect.

It was left for the radiologists, and anyone who worked within a hundred yards of them, to learn the hard way that their x-ray film stock was not only stupendously and whimsically volatile, but also *it didn't even need air to burn*! Old x-rays, when set afire, conveniently produce their own oxygen.

This bizarre fact was discovered by the firemen who responded to the disaster at the Cleveland Clinic. They noticed that the x-rays burned even better and produced even more poison gas when splashed with water from their fire hoses. In fact, the film would continue to flame boisterously and produce poison gas even when *totally submerged*!

120

The problematic stock began to be replaced with something less flamboyant in the '50s and now film itself is disappearing as radiology goes digital.

The MRI scanner is another radiological achievement that presents some unexpected dangers. Many startling surprises have occurred around these machines on account of the fact that few people realize the magnets are on *all the time*, even when the machine isn't in use.

Wandering too near the bore of an MRI has caused the following incidents:

The clip on a patient's aneurysm popped loose and they bled to death.

A policeman's gun was jerked out of his holster and went off.

A patient's knife slid out of a sheath strapped to his ankle and stabbed him in the abdomen.

An IV pole became a six-foot long stainless steel javelin.

Scissors and scalpels have flown about the room bayoneting bystanders—and at least once ending up in an MRI technician's head.

A German fireman fighting a blaze inside a hospital had the metal air tank strapped to his back sucked into an MRI, taking him with it and nearly strangling him to death before he could be extricated.

The unwary have been whacked in the head by computer monitors that unexpectedly went airborne. Office chairs, wheelchairs, hospital beds, oxygen tanks in all sizes, power tools, and industrial floor buffing machines have been sucked into the doughnut-shaped maw of the MRI, sometimes killing or seriously injuring hapless patients and bystanders.

Even turning an MRI machine off can be deadly if a situation referred to as a *quench* occurs:

The gases used to cool the magnets can give a technician and/or the patient and/or bystanders frostbite and/or asphyxiate them.

A tech might have only ten seconds to remove the patient and get out of the MRI suite before they will both be rendered unconscious.

One source recommended that in the event of a quench one should use a baseball bat to smash the window between the control room and the scanner before attempting to open the connecting door. One can only hope that a $20 wooden Louisville Slugger will be readily available should the most expensive and sophisticated device in the hospital begin to fail.

ROCK AND A HARD PLACE
Tough Cases

The practice of medicine requires extraordinary mental toughness and resilience.

Outcomes can be tragic. Patients die. And yet the physicians have to come back to work the next day, and the day after that.

Certain subspecialties have a much higher patient mortality rate than others. But one way or another, every doctor must learn to meet crushing situations with calm courage and a warm, positive outlook. If they can't, they burn out.

The following stories are about difficult cases.

What is That?

Dr. Davidson

"I am utterly baffled by something in an image almost every day. Things like thyroid nodules, for example. Everybody and their brother has them. Fifty percent of the population has them, and as you get older the percentage goes up.

"A small percentage of them can be cancer, but it's nearly impossible to tell the difference from a picture. The benign and malignant nodules look the same. By the time we can diagnose it from an image, it can be too late. So, if it's suspicious, you need a biopsy.

"Of the nodules that are biopsied, fifteen percent are removed. Of the nodules that are removed, five percent are cancer. But terrible things can go wrong in the surgery on a benign nodule.

"The cure rate for thyroid cancer is very high. Our ability to diagnose it has gotten better and better, but the percentage of patients who die from the disease has remained the same for many years."

VOMIT

Dr. Palmer

"A lady came in with left chest pain. They went looking for an embolism and took some images. They didn't find any emboli, but they noticed a thyroid nodule.

"In this situation there's an eighty-five percent chance you don't have cancer. But when the lady heard the word *cancer*, even though she had only a fifteen percent chance of having it, it created all kinds of stress and anxiety in her.

"Eventually the worry became unbearable and she decided to get a biopsy and have a surgical excision of the nodule. It turned out the nodule wasn't cancer, but during the operation a nerve was damaged and her vocal chords were paralyzed.

"This is one of the risks with this type of surgery, but now the woman couldn't speak or sing in the choir. Speaking is a fundamental human need and singing had been one of the primary pleasures of her life. These losses were terrible for her, but they were even worse for her husband.

"He was a veteran who had dementia. He was also hard of hearing. He ended up killing himself on account of the loneliness caused by his wife's inability to communicate with him.

"We have a term for this, it's VOMIT, which means Victim of Medical Imaging Technology.

"Everyone did the best they could, but still, this happened.

"Nodules in the lung, thyroid, or breast—most of them aren't cancer. As a radiologist you see the image and wonder, *What do I do with this? What should I say? Should I stress someone out for the rest of their life by mentioning this, or not?*

"You try to correlate the risk factors with the patient's primary care doctor and decide what's the wisest course of action. Unfortunately the immense bureaucratic system that has built up around healthcare overwhelms the doctors and triggers more and more aggressive interventions—and bad things happen during these interventions.

"As a neuroradiologist, I don't know as much about breast cancer as some other doctors do, but I know that issues around diagnosis and treatment are very controversial. Ductal carcinoma *in situ*, DCIS, pre-cancer or cancer— this diagnosis is going up, but, like in thyroid cancer, we're not sure if we're increasing life spans with our treatments.

"Even if you have thyroid cancer, if your immune system is good, your body can mediate it. Same thing with melanoma. Cancer can't let loose until something in the body allows it. Many cancers, if left alone, might involute and die on their own.

"With all our new imaging, we see *everything*. That's both good and bad.

"In the old days physicians got clues and hints from the images, but because they didn't have such great resolution of underlying disease and anatomy, they also looked at their patients carefully, using all their senses to come up with a diagnosis.

"Everybody has little bumps and nodules and things.

"With the new technology we're diagnosing more and more cancers, but for many types of cancer the mortality rate is not changing at all."

***

"Every human body changes, then adapts, and finally declines.
That's normal. That's life."

***

Spitting in the Ocean

Dr. Mayes

"One of my scrub techs had left us and was working as a roofer. He had an accident—he fell off a roof and got all busted up.

"He laid in a bed for a long time, healing. This was in the old days before trauma centers learned what happened to you if you laid in bed for a long time.

"It took years for us to understand that if patients laid around, they'd recover from terrible injuries, but silent clots would form in their veins, and when they stood up to go home the clots would float to the lungs and block the body's ability to get oxygen.

"We know this now, but we didn't know it back then.

"This fellow was being discharged and things started to go wrong. He was sent down to radiology to see if he was throwing a clot.

"We recognized each other, of course.

"I injected contrast medium into him and looked at my screen. The dye was showing me that almost every pulmonary artery he had was stopped up.

"It was a death sentence.

"I started getting rid of clots as fast as I possibly could. I knew that the way I was working on him was like spitting in the ocean, but I had to try like hell anyway.

"He was a *friend* of mine.

"I thought, if I can do this fast enough, maybe he can survive. The whole time I was working on him I shut off the back of my mind which was saying, *ain't no way.*

"He had very few symptoms, but he was a dead man.

"I couldn't save him.

"He died on the table.

"Nowadays they have filters they can put in to help catch clots, and they know not to let patients lay around so much. We learn things over time, usually the hard way.

"Medical care is always improving and when it does you look back and your heart breaks at your previous limitations.

"I wish we didn't have to learn this way. Some of the lessons are extraordinarily painful. You never get over experiences like that."

DNR

Dr. Stevens

"When I was an intern I had a female patient who had malignant hypertension. We had no treatment for it back then and they all died.

"I stayed up all night with the woman and regulated her blood pressure as well as I could by hand. There were four patients in a room and no room for chairs so I sat in one of the sinks between the beds to be near her IV pole.

"She was an unmarried lady. She had no family, nobody.

"Now the drugs for hypertension are much better. It's the same for ulcers—now we have medicine that works. And there are effective ways to treat heart attacks.

"It was terrible when there wasn't any way to for you to help your patients. The only thing you could do was sit with them and comfort them while they died."

Fatal Modesty

Dr. Langdon

"I see a lot of images of breast cancer.

"In one case I saw something suspicious on an image and told the patient she needed to get a biopsy. She did, and it came back as cancer.

"This lady didn't want to go to an oncologist and surgeon, though. She wanted to look for a natural cure. She disappeared for two years and we couldn't find her.

"She'd gone down to Mexico to get laetrile, an alternative treatment derived from ground up peach pits. Two years later she came back to us.

"We took new images and saw that she was now riddled with tumors. They were everywhere. You could hardly find a bone in her body that didn't have metastasis.

"There were nodules in her lungs and liver, as well as abnormal lymph nodes. It was very sad. When she was first diagnosed, her problem had been a single small tumor that was probably curable.

"This was an educated lady who'd had a good chance to live. We have a *lot* of options out there now.

"This is the most distressing kind of situation I see. The imaging technology enabled us to catch the disease early, but then the patient delayed treatment until it was too late."

"Before breast cancer awareness evolved, you would have women who would present for first time with a big mass in their breast. They wouldn't come in until they had an open sore where the cancer was ulcerating through the skin and the smell became unbearable.

"People get caught up in fear or denial and they don't do anything about their health. This is a *huge* problem, especially in women, and especially if the medical issue is in the breasts or vaginal area.

"I had a lady who didn't come in until her skin was an open sore from her shoulder to her sternum, from her clavicle to her rib cage. The mass was the size of two softballs and was emitting a foul smell.

"At this point the problem couldn't be fixed because so much skin was missing. She would've had to have skin grafts, but at this late date the doctors didn't think she'd survive the grafting procedures.

"This was also an educated lady. She'd been living with this for a long time, suffering in silence from a horrible condition.

"I understand where this behavior comes from. Women are trained from birth to be modest. They're told in the strongest possible terms that there are parts of a woman's body that *nobody* is supposed to see.

"It's an issue caused by our society. We've created women who are so modest they can't bear the thought of being seen by a doctor, even when they are suffering terribly.

"We should be more open about this. When these problems start, they're often relatively easy to take care of. They're certainly not something anyone should be ashamed of.

"But when the situation is allowed to progress, the problems become a lot more difficult to fix. It's very distressing when you see people for the first time and you realize it's already too late.

"Unfortunately this isn't as a rare situation as you might think. Most family doctors have seen these kinds of cases where female patients will conceal terrible pain and suffering for years, until it becomes unendurable, because it's in a so-called *private* area—then present for the first time with a catastrophic problem.

"We're killing women by instilling them with fatal standards of modesty."

***

"Medicine has no borders inside the body."

***

Past Distress

Dr. Travers

"I was looking at a patient in the scanner and realized I could see a hematocrit, a red blood cell volume, in the man's aorta. This shouldn't have been possible.

"When we take a CT we have a 3D photo. In this image, the patient was lying on his back. I could see that the blood in his aorta had settled. The red blood cells had drifted downward and the liquids up near his chest were becoming clear.

"For this to happen, the blood has to have been still for an extended period of time. This shouldn't be the situation in a blood vessel as important as the aorta.

"It could only mean one thing—the man had passed away in the emergency room and been brought to us for a test without anyone realizing he was dead. Structurally the patient looked fine, so he'd probably had a heart attack.

"It's awkward for the radiologist to be the first person to notice that the patient is dead, but it wasn't going to help him, or anybody else, for us to scan him at this point.

"I called the ER doctor to tell him. He thought I was mistaken, but I wasn't. The patient had been dead when he was transported from the ER to the scanner.

"You might think the technicians would have noticed this, or should have noticed it, but they often transfer unconscious or heavily medicated people. It's not unusual for patients to be nonresponsive to them.

"The techs wouldn't necessarily check for a pulse on a non-cooperative patient to notice that the person is past distress. Modern pulse oximeter sensors help prevent this situation."

Choking Up

Dr. Garcia

"The hardest part of the job for me is when I read cancer in a young person.

"I see cancer every day. I see so much of it, I've come to expect it.

"I tell myself we've all gotta go sometime. But when you see cancer in a child or a young pregnant woman, it's hard.

"Pregnancy causes physiological changes—hormone levels change, sometimes teeth will get looser, or cancers will spread. When this happens to a pregnant woman there are horrible ramifications for the whole family.

"I trained at St. Jude in Memphis. It was heartbreaking to see the cases there.

"I saw the mechanism of the disease and I came to appreciate the way we are made and the processes behind life in a human body. I also learned how things can go wrong.

"We are increasingly using scientific methods to divide everything into tinier and tinier little parts. That might make it easier to look at the pictures on a screen, like it does for kids shooting people in a video game, but as a radiologist, you're not playing a game—you're diagnosing disease, you're viewing human anatomy.

"I could distance myself if I wanted to. That way I would rarely need to interact with the patients and I could avoid sad situations. It's easy to step out of the reading room and talk to the referring physicians, but it's really hard to go talk to the families of one of these patients.

"I do it anyway.

"It's very difficult to speak with parents who are trying to decide whether they should discontinue care on their three-year old. But it's my job to try to help them understand that their toddler has horrible metastatic disease and that they should stop their doomed struggle to keep their child alive.

"In cases like this it's totally understandable that they would want to know what's happening, and they'd want to look at the images to evaluate the situation for themselves. But understanding the images isn't always simple for non-experts.

"I've spent many *many* years learning what's normal and what's abnormal. The images might look normal to the parents. But they're not.

"It's really rough. You get choked up.

"I go meet with them face-to-face and give them the information they need to make an informed decision. I try to convey what my training allows me to know. I'm a neuroradiologist. Brains and backs—that's what I see all day.

"'This is a bad situation,' you say, 'This is really, really bad.'

"I try to explain to them that their child has leptomeningeal disease. That it's metastatic and it's hard to treat.

"It goes to the surface of brain, so I try to explain, 'All these bright lines— if you don't understand, it looks good, but it isn't.'

"'Few things in a brain will enhance under imaging,' I say, 'but in this situation *everything* is homogeneously enhancing. There is diffuse abnormal enhancement.'

"But the parents have nothing to compare it to. So it's up to me to help them. That's the only way they have to understand what they are seeing.

"There are some things we don't yet know how to fix. It's very hard when one of these situations happens to a child, especially if it's your own child."

"When a terminally ill child is dying, things can sometimes get extremely unpleasant for the child in a way that is not necessary. That's a terrible situation to have to watch, and a terrible time for the little child to have to endure.

"The child will be having a series of cardiac arrests. They're trying to die, but are being resuscitated over and over because their parents refuse to accept what's happening.

"Eventually the child will finally manage to die, but it's not always a humane process. At times like this we have to make the decision to be merciful to the person who needs our mercy the most.

"And that's not the parents. We need to be brave and strong and wise and do what's best for the child, not what's best for ourselves.

"Some people are able to meet tragedy with courage and grace, and some are not."

Doctors Die

Dr. Anthony

"It's a documented fact that doctors die differently from ordinary patients. When confronted with a poor prognosis, physicians will often say, *I've had a good life*, and leave it at that.

"It's a personal decision, of course, about the patient's quality of life and the effect further treatments will have on the people around them. But it's a fact, doctors are less likely than other patients to have additional medical treatments or surgical procedures. And this applies to members of their families as well.

"I was always grateful that my mother lived long enough to see me get into med school and be successful with my studies so she knew I'd make a doctor.

"When she was dying things eventually progressed to the point where I had to take her to the hospital. Then, when she became unconscious, I stayed beside her all the time to prevent any extreme lifesaving measures from being performed by overzealous medical personnel.

"I was beside her when she stopped breathing.

"I knew how things worked in a hospital, so I didn't tell anyone. I sat there with her for fifteen more minutes so they wouldn't be able to do anything else to her.

"Then I went out to the nurses' station and told them."

Tough Situations

Dr. Michaels

"Some of toughest cases radiologists have to deal with involve child abuse. These situations are always very somber, exceedingly difficult.

"We see a lot of them.

"The hardest part is to be as objective as possible when looking at a study, any study. I always try my very best to do that.

"I don't want it ever to be a matter of, *Oh well, this area of hemorrhage might indicate this child was abused.*

"What matters is that I to try to figure out what's going on with the patient, and not worry about whether I am giving information that might be used to prosecute someone, or might cause someone to go to jail.

"We have a team here at the hospital that focuses on those issues. Their primary job is to investigate signs of potential child abuse. They're very good at their jobs.

"Unfortunately I work with them a lot. Especially on things like hits to the head, skull fractures, and brain bleeds.

"My job is to say what I see. I don't try to play detective. I don't try to act like I'm on *CSI* or something. I don't speculate about what caused what I'm seeing.

"Working here you notice that child abuse injuries are more common around the holidays. These patients don't typically come in with a label on them to indicate they're victims of abuse, but we see more of them around stressful times.

"Sometimes there's a witness, sometimes there isn't. Sometimes the child is having a seizure or acting sluggish and you see a hematoma or a fracture and you wonder what happened.

"You wonder how to keep the child safe.

"It's hard to bear."

Hard Work

Dr. Baxter

"Radiation has been used to treat cancer for over a hundred years, but it took a while for people to realize that radiation could *cause* cancer as well as *cure* it. Then it took a lot more years to develop good treatment protocols and better equipment.

"When I started in practice most of the cancer patients were pretty far gone by the time they got to us. Because of that it was very sad to work with them. Our imaging and treatment technology was not very effective back then and these were the days before chemotherapy was invented.

"We were treating people but we weren't doing them any good. The situations were so tragic, especially the kids. That really gets to you, when you can't help a kid."

Dr. Tate

"I've always worked in places with extreme poverty. I've spent my entire career in public hospitals. I've run ultrasound, OB/GYN, and neonatal in big inner city hospitals.

"I hang out in institutes where emergency care and congenital problems are common, but cancer, not so much. Some people deal with tragic situations better than I do.

"I've had to tell patients there are tumors. This is a hard thing to do. All cancers are sad. I wouldn't want to deal with cancer all the time."

Finding the Good

Dr. Page

"Sometimes you have to take a break to go out and see people having a good time.

"I'd find myself needing to go to the mall or the fair, or I'd need to go on vacation, just so I could see people who weren't sick or injured.

"If you see all that suffering all day long every day you have to get re-sensitized to people having a good time.

"Most people take that for granted, but I don't.

"When you see the kinds of things we see, you have to make an effort to enjoy every day, to find something good in every day."

Shaken Radiologist Syndrome

Dr. Franklin

"I was a pediatrician before I was a radiologist.

"One night I read an x-ray from the emergency room where a small baby had a bunch of broken ribs. He had other bones that had been broken, too. I could see old fractures that were healing.

"The child was brought in brain dead and, based on certain indicators like retinal hemorrhages and subdural fluid, he was identified as a shaken baby.

"I sat there for a long time looking at that x-ray.

"The radiologist who'd read this child's x-rays on an earlier visit to the hospital hadn't caught the previous fractures, probably because the baby had come into the ER during a busy time and the doctor was in a hurry and didn't notice them.

"It was sad because there were previous rib fractures that were actually displaced, not just faint white lines or cracks, but where the bones were moved out of visible alignment. My colleague hadn't ignored them on purpose, of course, but his brain had just passed them by.

"You see the breaks, but you don't perceive them. This is every radiologist's nightmare.

"It was an emotional situation. If he'd seen the fractures, maybe the baby would've been taken out of a violent environment and lived.

"You see terrible things done to babies. I had to leave pediatrics because I couldn't bear to see all the abused children. I was young and I just couldn't stand it.

"I switched to radiology because, to me, being a radiologist was sort of like being Sherlock Holmes. I wanted to solve mysteries, to figure out why a patient was feeling bad.

"I knew if I could make a diagnosis, I could help the doctor cure the patient. Only later did I realize I was I still going to have to see the same child abuse injuries in radiology."

Keeping the Patient in the Dark

Dr. Sergeant

"In many cases radiologists aren't supposed to tell the patient what they see. Communicating with the patient is often something the attending physician wants to do.

"The way we usually work is that we get requests to produce various kinds of images or do certain types of tests and we report our findings to the doctor who ordered them.

"Once I was reading an x-ray on a lady who worked at the hospital. I knew her. My kids knew her. She was a real pistol—funny, always making jokes.

"I read her chest x-ray and saw that she had a huge tumor in one of her lungs. I knew she was a smoker. She had the wrinkled skin and husky voice that told you that.

"When I saw the tumor I cried.

"Then I had to call her doctor and tell him so he could break the news to her. After I made the call I had to hide and avoid her because I wasn't allowed to tell her what I'd seen.

"I knew if she saw my face, I'd give it away. I knew she was going to die, but I didn't dare tell her."

"Over the years I had two occasions where I did a barium enema on a good friend and discovered a large colon cancer. Those kinds of situations really hit you hard.

"By the time they were tested, both of my friends had cancers almost as big as my fist. They had both ignored symptoms for a long time.

"Being a professional radiologist meant I had to tell the attending physician what I'd seen, not my friend.

"That was my job."

Proof of Life

Dr. Williams

"Radiologists get cases at the farthest extremes of life—at the very beginning and at the very end.

"We perform ultrasounds on expectant mothers. We're the ones who give the family their first look at their baby.

"And we also get cases that are at the end of life. We do the nuclear medicine studies for brain death.

"The end-of-life tests are always very challenging. The situations are very somber, especially because all of our patients here at St. Jude are children.

"We inject technetium into the bloodstream and look with a special camera to see if any of the chemical is getting to the brain. It's a very sensitive test. We do it to determine whether the patient's condition is completely incompatible with life.

"When we do the study the child's parents are nearby. An organ donation team might also be standing by. People are waiting for me to say whether it's appropriate to withdraw care such as a fluids, nutrition, or breath support, or, in some cases, whether it's time to proceed to organ donation.

"I will do this last test on the child to see if the damage might possibly be reversible. If the study reveals that no blood is getting to the brain, it will be the last test we perform on the child

"We do this when a formal legal decision has to be made. Here at St. Jude we do this test a lot. Most hospitals would not have to do it very often, but here this type of testing is an important part of my job.

"Children are so resilient. They are not little adults. They are very different from adults in many ways. They can recover from terrible injuries, even severe brain injuries.

"I've seen a child recover from a *big* stroke, a *huge* stroke. Children's brains are very plastic. So when you're doing this test you want to be absolutely sure there's no chance whatsoever for the child to recover. That's what we're testing for.

"Several physicians are involved. Before the child is brought down to radiology, a neurologist has already performed an EEG, a brain study, and he has confirmed that the patient meets the neurological standard for brain death. Then they come to radiology.

"If we can prove there's no blood flow to the brain, we can be certain there's no possibility the child could ever get well. Then, depending on the

142

situation and the parent's wishes, we will remove life support or allow the organ donation team to begin their work.

"It's an awful situation. And it's usually not the first time we've seen the child. When we have a patient sent down for a legal determination of brain death we've often had them here for a test before—when the initial injury occurred—like a stroke, or drowning, choking, a bad fall, or a car accident.

"But if we see there's no blood flow to the brain, we know we won't ever see this little child again."

"People are going to die, that's what medicine is.

"Because of my subspecialty and the place I work, I know that many of my patients will die. They are all children, so their deaths are particularly hard. I wish that none of them would die, but this not going to be the case, so I have to accept it as part of life.

"We are all going to die.

"When I'm in a situation where I know I can't beat it, I try to accept it. I try to not let the mortality in my field depress me. Instead I try to use it to motivate myself to work harder, to do better, and to drive innovation.

"Everyone has to die, but that doesn't mean we die in misery, or agony, or suffering without hope. We can have acceptance and be peaceful as we die."

Last Breath

Dr. Whitfield

"I was in the room when my mother died, when my daughter died, and when my father died. I was right next to each of them when they took their last breath.

"When my mother and daughter died, both times it was almost like I could feel something in the room, something coming off them, lifting up from their bodies. When my dad died, I didn't get that same feeling.

"But two times I could feel when the person died something palpable was happening. I felt something emanate from the person as they died, right before my eyes. I don't know how to explain it. There's nothing detailed I can say, but I've wondered about it ever since.

"I've been with a lot of people when they died. The moment of death is a weird moment and you have weird thoughts. I touched my daughter right after she died. I remember thinking, *This is as warm as she's ever gonna be.*

"When my daughter died, that was the hardest thing in the world, the worst experience of my life."

SKELETON KEYS
Living With Uncertainty

Imagine-omas

Dr. Daniels

"You can cause a lot of expense, a lot of injury, even *kill* someone with a recommendation of further action on something that might have been harmless if you'd left it alone.

"You can cause a similar disaster if you fail to mention a tiny blip on a image that will evolve into something much worse.

"These parameters are always on our minds. Images are often ambiguous and yet we have to make a determination on each of them, one way or another.

"We know we can kill our patients by either *under-calling* or *over-calling* a situation.

"Identifying little blips on a picture is not always easy. We have several slang terms for puzzling equivocal things that show up on images, words like incidental-omas, imagine-omas, or vague-omas.

"There are entire radiology conferences devoted to trying to understand what is reasonable to do when you see one of these. We struggle to decide which cases need further investigation, which ones need a biopsy, and which ones you should leave alone.

"It's a huge issue."

"A lot of people don't realize there are several types of foreign bodies that won't show up on an x-ray. You may or may not see wood inside a person. Some kinds of dirty wood you can see, but you can't see everything with an x-ray.

"There are some kinds of foreign bodies you can see with ultrasound that you can't see on a regular x-ray.

"A CT or an MRI might show more kinds of foreign bodies, but it's expensive to do those tests, and, even then, you still might not see anything."

***

"Ultrasound is basically just a fish finder."

***

Exploring

Dr. Harmon

"Radiological imaging can be a safer and cheaper alternative to surgery. That's an enormous advancement in diagnostics.

"Sometimes an injury or an illness couldn't have been discovered without imaging. Other times it couldn't have been discovered without surgery. And sometimes you do surgery on someone who doesn't need it. That's just how things work.

"In the past, the standard of care was that up to twenty percent of the patients sent to the operating room for removal of their appendix should turn out to have a normal appendix.

"If you weren't taking out a normal appendix every five or ten patients, you were being too conservative and you were going to miss a patient whose appendix would rupture before you dealt with the issue—and that's a severe problem. You don't want an appendix to rupture before you get in there.

"But now, with the improvements in imaging during the last fifteen or twenty years, the rate of operations on a normal appendix has been reduced from twenty percent to about two percent.

"That's a meaningful improvement.

"Exploratory surgery is barbaric. It used to happen a lot because that was the only way we had to find out what was going on. With all the imaging we have available now, though, almost nothing can hide from you.

"But just because we can see it, doesn't mean we can get to it.

"You can see things in certain areas of your brain or your heart that it will do more damage to get to than you'd solve when you arrive."

TMI

Dr. Forester

"Diagnostic tests and lab work aren't as accurate as people might think. And the significance of the information you get isn't always as clear cut as it's made out to be.

"You can die even though your blood values are perfect and all your images look fine. People do it every day.

"Conversely, there's almost always *something* to worry about on every film you read. You see a shadow that could *possibly* be something, like a tiny tumor.

"It's probably not, but you don't know for *certain*. You're never a hundred-percent sure.

"You can actually see *too much* now with CTs and MRIs. You might have a hundred different images displayed at the same time. You can get overwhelmed.

"The wonderful technological leaps in medical imaging mean that we now have TMI, too much information. Our human brains are overtaxed trying to make sense of all the computer-generated pictures.

"Computers are already being designed to interpret the massive amounts of data they generate. Someday, maybe not too far in the future, radiological images will be automatically self-interpreted.

"Colorful models of the patient will pop up and rotate in all three dimensions—and the machine that created them will also interpret them.

"We won't need radiologists to read images anymore."

So Many Pictures

Dr. Wakefield

"The use of imaging has gotten way out of hand. I've been asked to perform an ultrasound on a pimple. The referring physician was worried that there might be osteomyelitis under it. He wondered if the patient had picked at a bump and spread an infection to the bone.

"I was asked to do a bilateral mammogram on a nine-year-old boy. I wouldn't do it. I did an ultrasound instead. There's no radiation to the child that way.

"There's a huge cost of care, an enormous cost, and no one will talk about it. There's a massive over-utilization of imaging these days.

"I'll be asked to do ten thousand dollars worth of tests on a ninety-eight-year-old woman who's dying. They'll order brain tests, for example.

"I'll call the referring physician, and ask, 'What're you gonna do if it's positive?'

"'Nothing.'

"'Then we don't need to do the study,' I'll say.

"Sometimes we're treating the doctor more than the patient. Some of these exotic tests are being ordered solely because the doctor is curious.

"I've done expensive tests on DNR patients, people who've signed documents ordering us *Do Not Resuscitate* them, and I ask, 'What the heck are we doing this for?'

"The attending physician will say, 'We think she's bleeding somewhere.'

"'Are you going to operate on her if she is?'

"'No, an operation would kill her.'"

Referred Pain

Dr. McBride

"In medicine these days there's a pervasive fear of being sued. Unfortunately for radiologists, one of the prime factors in getting sued is whether or not the patient knows the doctor.

"You used to know your doctor and he knew you. You had a relationship and there was trust. Now that's changing.

"Radiologists are particularly vulnerable to this problem of not having a personal relationship with their patients. We're handicapped by a lack of rapport because of the way we work. We rarely see a patient in person, so they don't know us at all.

"And yet now, at a big hospital, nearly *everyone* gets an x-ray and a test. It's almost a hundred percent guaranteed. So we're doing work for every person who comes through the doors of the hospital. We don't know any of them, they don't know us, and if we miss anything, they'll come after us.

"In a big emergency room, if you come in with a bad headache you get a CT. Severe abdominal pain also gets a CT. That's because the doctor in the ER can't be sure what's wrong with you unless he orders the fancy test.

"The problem the ER doctor is dealing with is that your gallbladder can hurt you in your shoulder. Your appendix can hurt you in your stomach. Radiologists encounter this all the time. Pain is not necessarily felt at the place where the problem is.

"This phenomenon is called *referred pain* and it's very common."

The Smallest Patients

Dr. Pearson

"The entire field of pediatric neuroradiology is relatively new. There's not as much literature out there to refer to for guidance as there is in most fields. It's a good career choice for someone who likes challenges and who can cope with an area of medicine that is less mature than others.

"A lot of the things we're doing now and some of the diagnoses we're making wouldn't have been possible prior to the development of the MRI. We're paving our own path in this area of specialty. We're a small community and we share information with each other.

"To do this work, you have to be curious enough to try to figure out the answers to your questions and you have to be okay with a little uncertainty.

"One of the biggest challenges in pediatrics is working with patients who can't speak.

"In adult medicine, sometimes there's an easy answer to your question. For example, if you see a line on a bone and you can't be sure if it's a fracture or a blood vessel, when you're dealing with an adult, you can go to the patient and press on the place. If it hurts it's probably a fracture. If it doesn't hurt it's probably nothing.

"But if your patient is a kid, you can touch them where there's no fracture and they might squirm, or they might even squirm when you're not touching them at all.

"There are two competing concerns in pediatric neuroradiology.

"On a plain film you can't see as much as you can on a CT or an MRI, but a CT requires radiation, and radiation effects are probably more pronounced on young children. You'd rather not expose a child to radiation unless you have to.

"The child isn't exposed to radiation with an MRI, but an MRI can take maybe half an hour, and to get a good image, the patient has to hold still. There's a medicine we can use to sedate a child while we do the MRI, but you might not want to use that type of drug on a patient who is unstable.

"Fractures show up better on an MRI, but a CT is quicker and that technology is available twenty-four hours a day. If a child is brought in to the hospital in the middle of the night with a head injury you can do a CT, but that means you'll be shooting them in the head with radiation.

"So if it's not an emergency, if the patient can tolerate some delay, and the MRI can be scheduled within a reasonable amount of time, it's better to do

152

an MRI than a CT because then you don't have to give the child any radiation."

"I have a valuable talent for a person who works in pediatric radiology. I have the ability to get a small child to hold still.

"I can also make most very young kids be quiet with a high-pitched voice and singing. I got an anecdote about this in *Reader's Digest* in the section called *All in a Day's Work.*

"I'll sing a high-pitched tune and get the techs to join me in singing and that makes the whole room a happy place for the kid getting the exam. One of our techs was a professional singer.

"We sing *Ba ba boom, Wa waa waa,* or *B-I-N-G-O and bingo was his name O.* Or sometimes I use the sounds *Wooooo wooooo* to quiet the kids down.

"When I worked in New York, parents would ask for a CD of me singing to take home with them so they could play it and get their kids to be quiet."

"In the early days of ultrasound, we used to have to read the images live. We didn't have the ability to record anything and replay it. That meant I had to hit the *stop* button and freeze the image during a moment when the kid wasn't moving around too much.

"It was like playing a video game and I was really good at it.

"I did research when ultrasound was in its beginnings. I developed ultrasound diagnostic tests for newborns, so they didn't have to get any radiation.

"Pediatric patients, *peeds,* benefit from less radiation. These tests have been really helpful in patient care.

"I like technology. It's an extension of the physical exam.

"I like the fetus. I consider the fetus a pediatric patient. Eventually the American Academy of Pediatrics agreed with this idea and then the American College of Radiology did as well.

"In the first few months of life you can look at a baby's brain with ultrasound through the soft spot in their skull, if it's still open.

"The image looks like a bad snowstorm, but in your subspecialty training you spend a lot of time learning anatomy and the various disease processes. You become able to interpret the snowstorm image accurately."

Unclear Medicine

Dr. Chatterjee

"In radiology there are certain images that are more easily interpreted than others. Ultrasound images are confusing unless you've had experience working with them.

"Nuclear Medicine, a subspecialty that that uses small amounts of radioactive material to diagnose or treat patients, also produces images that can be difficult to read. It's just the nature of that technology that the pictures won't always be sharp.

"Radiologists sometimes jokingly refer to Nuclear Medicine as *Unclear Medicine.*"

"Ultrasound can give us *some* information, but it can be difficult to figure out what's going on from an ultrasound. Fortunately we can do fetal MRI now.

"Getting images of a fetus with an MRI is more challenging than for other patients because there's no way to stop the child from moving around. That means I'm shooting at a moving target. But we can use special ways of taking the picture on the MRI that are very fast, so we can negate some of the motion.

"Sometimes you can see an abnormality, but you don't know what it means. It might have minimal to no consequences later.

"We know that fetuses who have certain kinds of problems we can see on an MRI tend to also have other problems. But if we know about the situation in advance, when these babies are born we can take them straight to the operating room and fix them.

"Maybe the baby has abnormal blood vessels. If you know this ahead of time you can go in and fix the vessels immediately after the child is born. If you don't know it in advance, if you don't fix it before the baby is displaying symptoms of distress, the child will have serious heart problems afterwards.

"It's much better if you can find the problem while the baby is still asymptomatic. That way they have a much better chance to do well."

1, 2, 3, 4

Dr. Campbell

"When you're working on a case, you don't always realize how important your interpretation will turn out to be.

"I'd been in Memphis for just a couple of months and I was reading images on a child who was about four years old. She had a brain tumor. We looked at the MRI and saw the brain tumor and multiple metastatic deposits spread throughout the little girl's nervous system.

"She had an intraoperative MRI, a special setup in the operating room where they take images during surgery. Six months later she had a complication, and then six months after that she had another complication.

"I talked to the child's neurologist, then later I got a request to look at a study from St. Jude and give my opinion. I looked at it and said what I thought. It was a complex thing.

"If you see something new on an image, you don't know if it's related to the treatment, or if it's the tumor coming back. I said I thought it was related to the child's treatment, and afterwards that was confirmed to be the case.

"Then the same issue arose again with the same patient. That time, because of the uncertainty, they decided to do a biopsy. A biopsy on something in the brain is a serious procedure.

"I reviewed the radiological study with the child's parents. I told them what I saw. I explained why I thought what we were seeing wasn't a tumor coming back, but was being caused by the treatment. I hadn't realized the first, second, or even the third time I looked at the images taken elsewhere that all of them were of the same little girl.

"It wasn't the same issue over and over. Each time it was something different appearing in a different place, and each time it looked like a tumor, but it wasn't.

"You wonder how the same child could have survived not just *one*, but *two*, *three*, and then *four* times where you think there will be devastating consequences, and yet she bounces back each time.

"Every time you look at these kinds of images you ask yourself, *Is this a tumor, or is it something else?*

"I always want it to *not* be a tumor. I always want to be able to say, *This is not a tumor.* But I need to be right. It's important that I be correct.

"Things that might seem like minor decisions at the time can have a major impact on the patient's course of treatment, on the patient's life, and on the lives of the entire family.

"With this little girl, I didn't realize that I was helping with the same child every time, and also I didn't realize that our interaction would have such far-reaching consequences.

"The family started a foundation to take care of other families of patients with brain tumors. They were having a dinner and a silent auction to raise money for the foundation and I was invited.

"I'd just gotten married. When the time came, I'd had a really busy day and was tired, but my wife and I went to the dinner anyway. We walked in and the place was crowded with people who were getting signed in. The mother of the little girl was hosting the event. She saw me and stopped what she was doing and came over and gave me a hug.

"I've become involved with the foundation, GoLucyGo.org. They serve Thanksgiving and Christmas dinners at LeBonheur and gives assistance grants to help families in similar situations.

"I've been interacting with this little girl for a couple of years now and she's still alive."

"I see dozens of MRIs every day. For every one of them, there's a family waiting for the results. One or more physicians are waiting to hear my thoughts also, so they can come up with a treatment plan.

"Every single MRI is very, very critical. I work in a subspecialty area where I don't see a lot of normal studies.

"A very large percentage of what I see every day concerns brain tumor problems. LeBonheur is the biggest pediatric brain tumor center in North America. It does the surgery for St. Jude.

"More than most radiologists, I try to seek out interactions with other people. I go see the patient or their family. Sometimes a kid has a bump on their head and an MRI is requested. I'll go see the bump. It could be a lymph node, or a swelling, or a tumor.

"Before you get there you might think, *Oh, it's just a little bump. That's normal.* But when you see your patient in person, you experience the concern in the child's eyes and in their parents' eyes.

"Parents will often fear the worst. That's just human nature. So I go and see them. I talk to them in person. I try to help them as much as I can."

Being Human

"If your goal is to provide the best assistance, rather than simply going through a stack of x-rays, every time before you look at an image you remind yourself that this picture is of a human being who has a family that is very concerned about them."

Missing Things

Dr. Vaughn

"You miss things.

"In retrospect you realize that something wasn't what you thought it was. You realize you made an error.

"These things happen. Life can be capricious.

"In retrospect, you can see it, but you didn't call it at the time.

"Sometimes you misread life or death things.

"It tears your heart out when you see that you've done that.

"You remember those cases and feel distress about those patients for the rest of your life."

***

"Wisdom comes from experience. Experience comes from mistakes."

***

MIRACLES

Now You See It, Now You Don't

Dr. Hankins

"I had a motorcycle accident. I was able to crawl out from under the bike, but I needed surgery on the leg that was crushed.

"Before the operation I was laying there, groggy, while unbeknownst to me, my colleagues were back in a reading room reviewing my x-rays and discovering a three-centimeter mass in my chest.

"They didn't send just anybody to break the news to me. They had our top guy do it. When I saw who they'd they sent, I knew it was gonna be something bad. And it was.

"My mother had died of lung cancer, so ever since then I'd been afraid of getting it, too.

"I decided it would be okay to die of lung cancer, but thought I should get a biopsy and then take at least one shot at curing it. We had to wait until after the surgery on my leg to do anything about the mass, but when the leg had been dealt with, they took some more images of my lung.

"This time they sent the top guy in *again* to break the news to me about what they'd seen. That struck me as *extremely* ominous. I suspected the situation had gotten much worse during the delay.

"But instead of giving me bad news, he said, 'I think you need to come look at this x-ray.'

"I did, and the mass in my chest was completely gone. There was no longer anything there. Nothing at all.

"I wondered what had happened. Had it been a misread? Had we *all* been fooled? Several radiologists looked at the studies very closely and they all agreed that there was a mass in my chest shortly before, but now it was completely gone.

"That was a weird experience. It took a while for me to process it, but as I stood there looking at the new image it gradually hit me, *I'm gonna live!*"

Immunity

Dr. Jameson

"A friend of mine had carcinoma of the bladder and prostate. It was anaplastic, wildly growing, very malignant, and had spread to the lymph nodes and blood vessels.

"MD Anderson in Houston had treated eighteen similar cases and all of their patients died within eleven months. It was a very aggressive form of cancer.

"I sent my friend to Dr. Fray Marshall at Johns Hopkins where they performed an early, experimental type of surgery on him. They removed his bladder and prostate, did node dissections, and built him a new bladder out of part of his colon.

"He had surgery and chemo and now, twenty-eight years later, he's still alive and running around. He got a lot of help from doctors, but he also experienced a miracle.

"Somehow he was able to summon a burst of immunity from inside himself that the other patients hadn't been able to generate.

"It saved him."

Vanished

Dr. Eddington

"When I was working in Galveston I drained an abscess on a lady's neck and took a biopsy. It turned out to be cancer.

"We sent her to every consult, did everything we could, but we weren't able to find the primary tumor.

"In cancer therapy you don't want to design a patient's treatment around a secondary lesion. You need to find the primary site and work from there.

"'Let's start all over,' I said.

"We took another full history, did another physical, and repeated all the consults, but with no success. At that point, the best strategy I could think of was to grab one of the plastic surgery residents, and ask, 'Will you do a radical neck dissection on this lady?'

"Normally you would never do a significant surgery on a secondary tumor without knowing where the primary lesion was, but in this case we felt we had no choice.

"The plastic surgery resident agreed to operate on the woman and when he did, he discovered there was no tumor. They went back and pulled the original slides and studies for comparison and there was no question—there had been a cancer in the woman's neck, but now it was gone.

"The patient had successfully rejected her own tumor. That's the cure for cancer—you stimulate your own immune system to attack the tumor. This patient managed to save herself.

"You see cases like this every so often. They're mysterious—and miraculous."

Just Breathe

Dr. Linton

"I am a Christian. I believe miracles can happen. I've seen them with my own eyes.

"I was there when one of them happened to a fellow who'd intentionally overdosed on Tylenol. He'd was in liver failure and by the time I saw him he was on a ventilator.

"His heart would still beat as long as he had mechanical respiratory support, but all the other signs indicated he was brain dead.

"I reviewed the man's chart and learned that he'd struggled with depression for many years. In a moment of weakness it had become too much for him.

"The hospital wanted to confirm the man's condition before they removed life support. A neurologist did all the studies his department does at a time like this and he pronounced the man dead. Then the patient was sent to radiology.

"We were asked to perform a nuclear medicine study to see if there was any blood flow to the man's brain. We did the test and my boss at the time also pronounced the man dead. They unplugged the machines and went about preparing the patient for transport.

"Then, while they were working, the man started breathing again on his own!

"We were all deeply shocked, but also very happy. It was an extremely moving situation. I got to be present when a human being was given a second chance at life. It was a miracle.

"Afterwards I made an effort to keep track of his case and was told he was a different person after he came back. His mood was much better."

"Miraculous things happen every day. I know they do because there have been times in my own life when God has intervened.

"When I was six years old my dad and I were cleaning out a cabinet and he handed me a pistol to hold for a moment. He didn't realize the gun was loaded.

"Being a typical little boy, I pulled the trigger and the gun went off. But miraculously the pistol misfired. Instead of hitting my father, the bullet did a rare thing called a *squib load*.

"The bullet came out to the very edge of the barrel but then it stopped. You could see the tip of it sticking out.

"If the gun had fired normally, I would've shot my dad. I might've killed him and had to live with that for the rest of my life. But it didn't. The bullet stayed inside the gun.

"That was a miracle."

Twin Vision

Dr. Greene

"I experienced a miraculous event during my junior year of college when I was on spring break. It was a Saturday morning, about 7:30, and I'd been up all night the night before. I should've been sleeping soundly, but I wasn't. Instead I was having a vivid dream.

"In my dream I was driving a white Mercury Topaz like the one my twin sister and I shared. I approached a convenience mart with a gas station that was a mile or so from our house.

"In the dream there was a little bit of haze and drizzle, so I slowed down as I drove past the store. A guy in a truck pulled out really fast and rear-ended my car.

"Fortunately I had my seatbelt on, so I wasn't seriously injured, but I got whiplashed. The dream was so real I actually jumped out of bed while still half-asleep. My left shoulder was hurting where a seat belt would've been.

"Since I was up, I went to the bathroom and, as I came out, my mom saw me. Apparently I looked odd, because she asked me, 'Are you okay?'

"I told her what had happened. Then I went back to bed, intending to go back to sleep. A few minutes later I heard the phone ringing.

"It was my sister. She'd had an accident on her way to work. She told my mother almost exactly the same story I'd told her minutes before. The only discrepancies between the two accounts were that she was driving the Topaz instead of me and the color of the truck that hit her was different from what I'd seen in my dream.

"The accident happened at the same spot, at the same time, everything, that I'd seen in my dream. My mom was freaked out.

"I asked how my sister's shoulder was. She said it was fine. She had no whiplash or shoulder pain.

"Had my mom not been a witness to this, later I would've thought I'd imagined the whole thing. But I told my mom all the details before it happened, and she told my sister during that first phone call, so all three of us knew about it. There were multiple confirmations that this actually happened.

"That shows you that there are possibilities out there that we normally don't take into account. When life circumstances become difficult, it's good to remember things like that."

Survival

Dr. Vanhook

"I did a barium enema on a patient and we discovered he had colon cancer that was already at stage four.

"Additional studies and surgery confirmed he had metastatic nodules in his liver, neoplastic spread to the lymph nodes and mesentery, nodules like little grapes throughout his liver, and two nodules in his right lung.

"At the time this fellow was sixty-nine years old. He was in a tough situation, but he decided to try for a cure and have the tumors surgically removed.

"It was a good decision. He lived twenty more years and when he died at age eighty-nine, it was not from cancer, but from heart disease.

"The doctor's did their part, but I feel sure somebody at a higher level had a hand in that man's survival. Somehow, after surgery, his body was able to reduce the tumor insult to such an extent that his own immune system could squelch the remaining metastatic disease.

"He had a miraculous recovery. This proves that you just never know how things will turn out. No one can ever forecast the course of any patient's disease with absolute certainty. There's always a chance for a miracle."

Walking Wounded

Dr. Manning

"Do I believe in miraculous cures? Sure.

"I believe there is something other than us guiding things. I've seen it firsthand.

"When I was an intern a guy came in with a lung cancer that had grown all the way through his chest wall and erupted to the outside. I biopsied it myself.

"We gave him a little radiation and a little chemo, but not enough to do him any good. Then I went away to the military and was gone for several years.

"One day after I'd returned, I looked up and saw that same guy come walking by. I was shocked. He shouldn't have been alive.

"I pulled his most recent images and looked at them. The tumor was gone. He'd been cured.

"Now that was a miracle.

"There have been many times when I've seen patients with tumors that were inoperable, cases you'd think were hopeless. In tough cases like these the images will often get sent around to different places, to get different opinions.

"I work at St. Jude and Le Bonheur which means that many of our patients are coming to us after a dozen top places have already said the tumor was inoperable.

"I've looked at the MRIs and sat with the neurosurgeons on a lot of these extremely difficult cases. The surgeon will say, 'If we operate on that, the patient will lose the use of the right side of their body,' or 'After the operation the patient won't be able to talk,' or 'It won't be possible for me to reach that with my instruments.'

"So we sit there together and we talk. We try to come up with a plan to get a full cure of the tumor without any complications.

"After doing this for years I know from experience that you mustn't write anyone off. You never give up hope.

"If you didn't already know that, you learn it here. You see a person who you would think had no chance to survive. But then, all of a sudden, they get cured.

"You never write anyone off. *Never.*"

"Have I seen miracles? Yes.

"And I've certainly been at a loss for words more than once. There have

168

been times when everyone is just stunned—we look at each other and say, 'Wow. What are the odds?'

"A lot of miracles aren't flashy. They're not accompanied by trumpets or a bright light.

"Many miracles are performed by people who are doing their jobs. Human hands are performing the miracles.

"But that right there *is* the miracle."

ACKNOWLEDGMENTS

I'm deeply grateful to the physicians who generously shared some of the most memorable moments from their careers. This book is my heartfelt tribute to them and the tens of thousands of radiologists who patients may never get to meet.

Dr. Asim Choudhri
Dr. Harris L. Cohen
Dr. Bruce R. Crossman
Dr. Lloyd C. Davis
Dr. R. Ian Gray
Dr. George W. Kabalka
Dr. Mohammad K. Khan
Dr. Randall A. Loy
Ann Robbins-Phillips
Dr. Linnea J. Priest
Dr. William Webster Riggs, Jr.
Dr. Charles E. Walbroel
Dr. William L. Walls
Dr. Daniel K. Westmoreland
Dr. Dennis G. Westmoreland
Dr. Paul T. Wooten

This book is dedicated to the memory of Dr. Jay Watson Maxwell, a classmate of my father's who was a legend in our family for building a callus across his chest during medical school from leaning against his desk for such long hours, studying—after being threatened with expulsion if he didn't improve his grades.

Jay not only let me sit in the pilot's seat of a fighter jet when I was a child but he also introduced me to the magic of the radiology reading room. I will never forget him.

There is a small companion book to this volume, *Talking to Skeletons: Behind the Scenes with a Radiologist*. It is a narrative that chronicles my fifteen years of intermittently shadowing one radiologist while he worked. Visit CarolynJourdan.com to hear her read stories from her books.

ABOUT THE AUTHOR

HOW YOU CAN HELP
Your reviews are extremely important in helping other readers locate this book. Please leave a review on Amazon and/or GoodReads.

BOOKS BY CAROLYN JOURDAN

Memoir
Heart in the Right Place * *Wall Street Journal* Bestseller *

Medical
Medicine Men: Extreme Appalachian Doctoring * *Wall Street Journal* Bestseller * Amazon All-Star *
Nurse: The Art of Caring
Radiologists at Work: Saving Lives with the Lights Off
Talking to Skeletons: Behind the Scenes with a Radiologist

Mystery
Out on a Limb: A Smoky Mountain Mystery * *USA Today* Bestseller * Best Kindle Book of the Year *
School for Mysteries: A Midlife Fairy Tale Adventure
School for Psychics: A Midlife Fairy Tale Adventure

Bears
Bear in the Back Seat: Adventures of a Wildlife Ranger Vol. I * *Wall Street Journal* Bestseller * Audible Bestseller *
Bear in the Back Seat: Adventures of a Wildlife Ranger Vol. II
Bear Bloopers: True Stories from the Great Smoky Mountains National Park
Dangerous Beauty: Stories from the Wilds of Yellowstone
Waltzing with Wildlife: 10 Things NOT to Do in Our National Parks

Writing
How to Write, Edit & Publish Your Memoir: Advice from a Bestselling Memoirist

ABOUT CAROLYN JOURDAN

Carolyn Jourdan is a *USA Today*, *Audible*, and 5-time *Wall Street Journal* bestselling author of memoir, medicine, wildlife, and mystery.

Jourdan's trademark blend of wit and wisdom, humor and humanity have earned her high praise from Dolly Parton and Fannie Flagg, as well as major national newspapers, the New York Public Library, Elle and Family Circle Magazines, and put her work at the top of hundreds of lists of best books of the year and funniest books ever.

Her wildlife books are listed in:

- *Top 10 Must-Reads That Could Save Our National Parks and the Environment* with John Muir, Henry David Thoreau, Lewis & Clark, Bill Bryson, and Ken Burns.
- *Top 50 Must Reads for the 100th Anniversary of the National Park Service* with Edward Abbey, Nevada Barr, and C.J. Box.
- *15 Books Every Healthcare Professional Should Read* by Physicians Weekly

Her books have been honored with citywide reads.

Carolyn is a former U.S. Senate Counsel to the Committee on Environment and Public Works and the Committee on Governmental Affairs. She has degrees from the University of Tennessee in Biomedical Engineering and Law.

She lives on the family farm in east Tennessee, with many stray animals, including a rescue Havanese named Jimmy.

Visit Carolyn at http://carolynjourdan.com
https://www.facebook.com/carolynjourdan
https://www.facebook.com/carolynjourdanauthor
https://www.twitter.com/carolynjourdan
https://www.amazon.com/Carolyn-Jourdan/e/B001JP1U4A/

Made in the USA
Coppell, TX
28 August 2022

82225062R00105